AUSTRIA

P.Buin
△

P.Linard
△

Val Tuoi

Val Tasna

SCUOL

chestra

Val d'Uina

LOWER ENGADINE

ZERNEZ

Val S-charl

PARK

NATIONAL

OFEN PASS

Val Müstair

usauna

S

P. Languard
△

ITALY

ina

BERNINA
PASS

Palü
△

Val Poschiavo

D0206058

Walks in
the Engadine
Switzerland

Lägh da Cavloc (Cavolocciosee) and Piz dei Rossi

WALKS IN THE ENGADINE
SWITZERLAND

by
KEV REYNOLDS

Cicerone Press
Hunter Publishing Inc.

Published in the U.K. by Cicerone Press, 2 Police Square,
Milnthorpe, Cumbria.   ISBN 185284 003 X

Published in the U.S.A. by Hunter Publishing Inc.,
300 Raritan Center Parkway, Edison, N.J.
ISBN 1-55650-081-5

In memory of 'Noldi' Feuerstein (1937-1981)
friend and colleague
an Engadine man all his days.

CONTENTS

Acknowledgements

I have known the Engadine Valley for more than twenty years and in all seasons, having had the great good fortune not only to spend many holidays walking and climbing throughout the region, but also to work there, watching the seasons mould one into another; skiing in winter, wandering the valleys and climbing the mountains in spring, summer and autumn. As a consequence, over the years I have become indebted to a number of people for their kindness, generosity and assistance. In compiling this guide I am reminded of this background of generosity, and gratefully acknowledge in particular the help given by the following individuals and organisations: the late 'Noldi' Feuerstein, mentor, colleague and friend who first introduced me to the Engadine; Myrta and Jörg Dössegger-Feuerstein for their friendship, hospitality and encouragement; to Alan Payne and Nigel Fry for sharing my rope on snow peak and glacier; to the many helpful people manning the valley's tourist information offices who patiently answered my questions; to the Schweizerischer Bünd fur Naturschutz for specific assistance with information regarding the National Park. And last, but by no means least, to my wife and daughters who have shared so many valley, forest, lake and riverside walks and whose company has added another dimension to this lovely landscape. This book is also theirs.

Tailpiece sketches by R.B.Evans

INTRODUCTION

Lying in the south-eastern corner of Switzerland, the Engadine Valley forms a 94 kilometres long trench that offers some of the finest walking in the Alps. Here there is something for everyone: gentle valley strolls ideal for a family outing, craggy 'middle-mountain' walks for the more adventurous, high-level routes that lead across glaciers and snowfields and rough passes for the experienced mountain trekker. There are dazzling lakes that make tempting picnic sites. There are forest walks where deer may be spotted leaping through the vegetation. There are high pastures with ancient hay barns linked one with another by narrow trails, and snow peaks glistening all around.

It's a high valley. A valley of contrasts. In the Upper Engadine, that is to say the area between Maloja in the south-west and Cinuos-chel, the valley has a number of large lakes spread across its floor. These lakes lie at an altitude of around 1,800 metres, while above rise big mountains with snowfields and little glaciers, alp pastures and cable-cars swinging to lofty perches with vast panoramas - winter playgrounds and summer wonderlands. Nearby, the snow giants of the Bernina Alps: shapely mountains like Piz Palü, Bellavista, Piz Roseg and Piz Bernina.

In the Lower Engadine, which runs north-eastwards and steadily loses height between Cinuos-chel and Martina, the valley narrows. In places the Inn river squeezes through tight gorges, wild and foaming in cataracts; a white-water river. But while the river often digs itself into these gorges, the valley itself is a green and verdant land, not a dark and mysterious one. There are forests clothing the lower slopes, but then rich meadowlands ease back, bedecked with flowers and attractive villages on the hillsides some way above the main valley road. The mountains here are quite different. Mostly they are bare of snow in summer; grey turrets rising from a world of green.

But from the main Engadine there run other valleys, too. Each has its own individual flavour. Each one broadens the walker's opportunities. In the south, for example, at the valley's head where the lake of Sils gives way to meadows and the little township of Maloja, there is a sudden drop over the Engadine's lip of Maloja Pass into a deep valley filled with the soft air and warmth of Italy. This is the Val Bregaglia, still Swiss but running into Italy and absorbing the atmosphere of that neighbouring country. It's an utterly charming region with delightful glens slicing into it that in turn are topped by great jagged peaks and granite walls like those of Piz Badile and Cengalo. On summer-bright hillsides are perched unspoilt villages - among the loveliest in all the Alps.

Branching away from the Upper Engadine to north and south are other little valleys worth exploring; Fedoz, Fex, the narrow wedge of Champagna, Suvretta and the modestly lovely Val Susauna. There's the broad shaft of Val Bernina that leads to that other intrinsically Italianate valley of Poschiavo, deep below the Bernina Pass. From it paths carve away through side valleys like those of Roseg and Morteratsch into a world of glaciers and permanent snow; into the heartland of the Bernina peaks, classic snow and ice mountains that rear into deep blue skies and impose their will on the surrounding country.

The Lower Engadine has its fair share of delightful side valleys, too. These may not be so well-known as those of the upper valley, but they're no less charming for all that. Val Tuoi behind Guarda is a classic case. At its head rises the great lump of Piz Buin across whose ridge runs the Austrian border where the Vorarlberg and Tyrol merge in the Silvretta group of mountains. The Silvretta in turn runs astride the Austro-Swiss frontier. Then there's the Val Sinestra, heavily forested lower down, but opening to pastures and seemingly lost villages deep within. And there's the S-charl valley, too, right on the edge of Switzerland's only National Park. That Park comprises a number of fine valleys; it occupies a rather special region. The National Park is contained solely within the boundaries of the Lower Engadine. There, man has a very low priority. There the world of nature is left to establish itself without his moulding influence. Walkers are admitted within certain restrictions, and wandering through valleys of this National Park, one senses a unique atmosphere; an untroubled calm. That alone makes a visit to the Engadine worthwhile.

Perhaps the Engadine is best known as a winter playground. With international resorts like those of St. Moritz, Pontresina and Scuol, and with such classic ski grounds as those of Corvatsch near Silvaplana, and Diavolezza and Lagalb in the Val Bernina; and the world-renowned Cresta Run hurtling between St. Moritz and Celerina, this is hardly surprising. But as grand as the Engadine most certainly is in winter, both summer and autumn are magnificent seasons for walker, climber and general lover of fine mountain scenery. There's colour and fragrance all around. There are wild flowers in profusion, and an abundance of wild life that is as rich and varied as any other alpine region can boast. Observant walkers who go

Tarasp Castle, Lower Engadine

quietly into the mountains will be rewarded by the sightings of red or
roe deer, of chamois, marmots or even ibex. There are mountain
hares, foxes and red squirrels. There are buzzards and eagles and
alpine choughs, capercaillie and woodpeckers and numerous finches
to be seen.

The walker's experience in the Alps goes far beyond the basic one of
wandering through a series of magnificent landscapes.

One of the pleasures comes from visiting little olde-worlde villages
and alp hamlets unaffected by the passage of time, apparently
unmoved by the technological age that has revolutionised the lowland
world. The Engadine and Bregaglia have their fair share of these, as
well as the hybrid abstractions of jet-set resorts like St. Moritz. On
hillsides remote from the world of fashion houses and discos, the
walker will come upon scenes snatched from *Heidi* almost everywhere.
Wonderful belvedere villages like Soglio in the Bregaglia. Tiny
collections of houses such as Grevasalvas and Blaunca above Maloja;
Isola perched beside the tranquil waters of the Silsersee (Lake of Sils);
Guarda and Ardez in the Lower Engadine, their romantic *sgraffito*
ornamentation picked out in the plaster of their walls; old Scuol with
its fabulous square; Tarasp with all the brilliance of its window boxes
and its castle atop a rocky pinnacle; S-charl tucked away from the

9

world and surrounded by dashing streams and green pastures. And high on the pastures themselves, the summer-only hamlets where peasant farmers graze their cattle and goats and make cheese as they have done since time immemorial. Plan Vest and Tombal are magnificent examples. Timber and stone constructions with flat slabs of quarried stone on their roofs and tiny windows that look out across napkin-sized meadows, out beyond the empty drop of mountainside to distant peaks like granite teeth on the skyline, often divorced from the lower valleys by wisps of cloud. A world above the world.

All these things are available and waiting for the walker in the Engadine and adjacent valleys of Switzerland.

Approach to the Engadine

Regular flights by Swissair between the U.K. and Switzerland are operated in conjunction with British Airways. Scheduled routes are from London (Heathrow) to Geneva, Basle or Zürich, as well as services from Manchester and Dublin.

Air services from North America fly to Geneva and/or Zürich from Boston, Chicago, Los Angeles, Montreal and New York. Those airlines that maintain a service across the Atlantic are Swissair, Trans World Airlines, Air Canada and Pan American.

Zürich will be the most convenient airport for visitors to the Engadine. The Flughafen is only a short bus ride from the centre of town, and most buses connect with the Hauptbahnhof (the main railway station) where trains run regularly to Chur, at which station you must change for the last leg of the journey by rail to St. Moritz, Pontresina or elsewhere in the Engadine. To those for whom monetary considerations are of secondary importace, private air charter can be arranged to fly in style from Zürich to the valley's airstrip at Samedan.

By rail the journey from Britain to the Engadine is a straightforward one. In summer there is a once-a-day through-train from Calais, but at other times the routing is the same: Calais-Basle-Chur-Samedan. On arrival in the Engadine at Samedan there are alternatives available. Either continue up-valley as far as the railhead of St. Moritz; down-valley via numerous villages to Scuol; or across to the Val Bernina for Pontresina, Bernina Pass and the Val Poschiavo.

For those who might already be in the Alps, there is the scenically spectacular 'Glacier Express' which links Zermatt with St. Moritz. Coming from Austria there is a train and bus link with Innsbruck via Landeck. There are trains from Italy via Tirano and the Val Poschiavo, and Postbuses coming from Como.

By road there is a first-class network of motorways through Switzer-

Guarda in the Lower Engadine

land these days which, upon payment of s special motorway tax -either arranged beforehand, or paid at the point of entry into the country - enables a fast journey to be made through the mountains. Chur is the key town to aim for. From there one can drive via Lenzerheide and Tiefencastel over the Julier Pass (2,284m) which is usually open throughout the year, and which brings you into the Upper Engadine at Silvaplana. From Chur an alternative drive, on a road that is more narrow than the Julier and closed in winter (November to late May), goes by way of Tiefencastel and Bergün over the Albula Pass (2,312m), arriving in the Engadine at La Punt, between Bever and Madulain.

Approaching the Lower Engadine, one would normally opt for the Flüela Pass (2,383m) which is closed from December to late May. This route comes from Landquart, some 14 kilometres north of Chur, and travels through Klosters and Davos before crossing the Flüela to Susch in a sharp elbow bend in the Lower Engadine.

Transport in the Engadine

Switzerland's first-rate public transport system is of enormous value to the walker. From a single valley base he can travel to any one of a number of locations by bus or train to begin the day's walk. Or if a walk should begin from the valley base, there will invariably be a convenient means of returning at the end of the day.

The *Rhaetian Bahn,* which is the railway system for the Canton of Graubünden (or Grisons), serves much of the valley. Frequent trains run from St. Moritz Dorf at its highest point, to Scuol in the Lower Engadine. Between the two there are many village stations. A second line runs from Samedan (and St. Moritz) through the Val Bernina via Pontresina to the Poschiavo Valley and on to Tirano in the Italian Valtellina. It's a delightful scenic journey, and along the route there is only one village before the Bernina Pass, but tiny stations conveniently situated at the mouth of several valleys, thereby making them easily accessible to both walker and climber.

On the side of each carriage a name-plate is fixed listing the destination, thereby ensuring that you board the correct train. For travel beyond the valley, two standards of train will be advertised: *Personnenzug* (a slow train stopping at practically every station along the way) and *Schnellzug* (an express). A *Schnellzug* generally offers a better standard of comfort in the carriages. Trains running through the Engadine and Bernina valleys are nearly all *Personnenzugs.* They are supremely punctual.

Postbuses are as predictably punctual as the railways. These

Village Square, Scuol - Lower Engadine

yellow buses, run by the Postal Service, are seen almost everywhere there is a road in Switzerland; an important means of communication and a veritable life-line for some of the more remote villages. While the *Rhaetian Bahn* goes no further than St. Moritz in the Upper Engadine, the Postbus continues along to the head of the valley, down the Maloja Pass to the Bregaglia and on into Italy. Services run over all the surrounding road passes. In some instances smaller buses meet the main through-valley Postbus to ferry passengers up particularly narrow and winding roads to serve isolated villages like Soglio and Guarda. They also run into the wild inner valleys like that of S-charl, and provide an important link throughout the region.

Whilst they mostly serve villages and towns, there are certain strategic points without habitation where a Postbus sign (*Haltestelle*) indicates a bus stop where passengers may be picked up on request. Other than at these specific points, passengers must buy their tickets not on the the bus itself, but at the Post Ofice where the bus is to be met. By pre-purchasing tickets in this way, the driver is able to maintain his schedule.

There are several cable-cars in the Engadine region that the walker can use to his advantage. They are uniformly expensive, but worth taking on occasions. Between St. Moritz and Sils Maria there are a

13

number on both sides of the valley. Val Bregaglia has one, from Pranzaira above Vicosoprano to the Albigna dam - convenient for reaching the Albigna hut. The Val Bernina has one leading to Diavolezza, another that goes to Piz Lagalb, and a chair-lift behind Pontresina. Nearby a funicular runs up the hillside to Muottas Muragl where there is a superb view of the Upper Engadine. A number of fine walks trace away from this point. Across the valley from Muottas Muragl, Celerina boasts a gondola lift to Marguns in the Val Saluver.

In the Lower Engadine, Ftan has a short-journey chair-lift, and from the top of this a high-level path leads round to Motta Naluns, which is served by gondola lift from Scuol.

Languages Spoken
The Engadine is a valley with a wide linguistic range. For most tourist purposes, of course, English will be generally understood; in hotels, some restaurants, railway stations, Post Offices, campsites, Youth Hostels etc. But not everywhere.

In a country with four official languages: German, French, Italian and Romansch, the Engadine uses three of them. Only French is the odd one out. Romansch is an ancient Latin-based language spoken by only one per cent of the Swiss population, but it is the traditional language of the valley. In the Lower Engadine it is a living language today, taught in schools - as it is in the Upper Engadine - and used daily in the home and at work. Thus it is that the map gives different names and different spellings for some of the villages, valleys or mountains.

German is more often heard in regular conversation in the Engadine, while Italian is predominant in the Bregaglia, from Maloja down. The names of villages clearly indicate this.

It might be helpful here to add a note of explanation with regard to the greeting given throughout the region covered by this guide indeed, it is used almost universally throughout Switzerland. It is used when walkers pass on a mountain path, or in meeting peasant farmers among the higher alps as well as in shops in the valley. Almost everyone uses the common *Grüetzi*, a shortened version of the proper German greeting of *Grüss Gott*, meaning 'God go with you'. In meeting more than one other, this greeting becomes *Grüetzi mittenand*.

Accommodation
There should be no difficulty in finding suitable accommodation anywhere in the region covered by this book. The Swiss have a long tradition of hotel keeping, and the Engadine and neighbouring valleys

have plenty of every standard of lodging to meet the needs of holiday makers no matter what their financial resources might be. It is quite possible to enjoy a very fine walking holiday in Switzerland without spending a small fortune. There are campsites in plenty, and Youth Hostels and modestly priced *pensions*. Naturally there are extremely grand hotels, but there are also intermediate hotels and, of course, mountains huts in the high regions that are basically for climbers, but for those attempting some of the more taxing walks included in this guide, they would be useful for overnight lodging.

For valley-based accommodation, the tourist information office of each small town and village will be able to supply a list giving the full range available, from the cheapest to the most expensive. The Swiss National Tourist Offices should also be able to give ready information. Their addresses are given under Appendix A. General details of accommodation available will be given elsewhere within these pages under the individual headings of particular valley sections. But perhaps a word or two might be in order with regard to off-site camping, the use of Youth Hostels and mountain huts.

Camping: Official campsites exist along the length of the Engadine and Bregaglia. A few of these offer just basic facilities, while others have not only first-class toilet and shower blocks, but are also equipped with laundry and drying rooms. Off-site camping is officially discouraged in Switzerland. Although it may be possible - and even permissible - to pitch a small tent overnight above the treeline, it should always be borne in mind that in these mountains grass is a valuable crop and every effort should be made to avoid damaging it. It should therefore never be automatically assumed that an apparently deserted piece of meadowland would be acceptable as a campsite. The moral is clear; if you feel determined to camp wild, please be discreet, and ask permission wherever possible. All camping and bivouacking is strictly forbidden within the boundaries of the National Park.

Youth Hostels: At the time of writing there are five Youth Hostels in the area covered by this book. They belong to the SJH *(Schweizerischen Jugendherbergen)* which in turn is affiliated to the International Youth Hostel Federation. Anyone holding a current membership card of the Hostels Association of his own country can therefore use hostels in Switzerland, provided there is space. Visitors wishing to take advantage of the hostels in the Engadine and Bregaglia are advised to join their own association before leaving home. Emergency membership in Switzerland is very expensive.

Many of the hostels throughout the country are being dramatically upgraded to a very high standard. The five spread along the Engadine and Bregaglia are of varying qualities. Those at St. Moritz and Pont-resina are lavishly appointed, while the little farm building at Val Susauna - the oldest Youth Hostel in Switzerland - is primitive in the extreme. But utterly charming for all that, with an atmosphere all its own. How much longer it will remain such an anachronism is quest-ionable.

Dormitory accommodation is offered in all. Meals may be provided at some, if not all of them, but those used to hostels with a tradition of self-catering facilities, will be disappointed to find in several of these there are either no kitchens available for members' use, or that self-cooking is actively discouraged.

Mountain Huts: Primarily, huts of the SAC *(Schweizer Alpen Club)* are intended as overnight shelters for climbers preparing for an ascent of a neighbouring peak. They are not provided as simple hotels in a wild setting, and should not therefore be used as such. There is a priority list for their use, but in practise few if any are ever turned away. Since this guide is mainly concerned with walking outings of a day's duration, it is assumed that few will need to spend a night in a mountain hut. But some of the routes described specifically visit huts as a point of interest, while others are linked together to create multi-day tours in which huts will necessarily be used. In such cases, their use is acceptable.

Those familiar with the mountain hut system in the Alps will need to read no farther, but for the first-timer it might be considered helpful to direct a few words. Firstly, mountain huts vary consider-ably in their standards of accommodation, if not in the basic facilities offered. In recent years some of those in the Bernina and Bregaglia mountains have been substantially renovated, enlarged and improved to a surprisingly high degree. Those who might have read reports about primitive conditions in the past will be delighted to find these have now got flush toilets and even hot showers!

Sleeping quarters are invariably of the *matratzenlager* variety; dormitories with a large communal platform on which a plentiful supply of mattresses, blankets and pillows are distributed. There is no segregation of the sexes. If the hut is busy, this type of sleeping arrangement can very soon lose any attraction it might otherwise have. On arrival at the hut and finding sufficient room, it is best to lay claim to your bed space by making it whilst there is light.

Most huts have a guardian who will allocate bed space and often provide meals. These can either be substantial in quantity and quality, or meagre and uninteresting, depending upon the interest and enthusiasm of the man in charge, and how recently supplies were brought up from the valley. Bottled drinks are usually on sale. In some cases - at Diavolezza, for example - there is no natural drinking water available, and in order to take some onto the mountain with you, it will become necessary to buy it by the litre from the guardian who will have boiled some for this purpose in the evening. Most huts, though, will have a spring nearby with water from it piped to the hut.

Staying in mountain huts is not cheap. The buildings are expensive to build and to maintain, and the cost of supplying them with food and equipment is aggravated by the distance everything must be transported from the valley. Hence the relatively high charges made. But if you plan to undertake one or two multi-day tours in the mountains, the special atmosphere that comes from staying overnight in such remote lodgings will make the experience worthwhile.

Flowers of the Valley
Any mountain walking holiday undertaken in Switzerland between mid-June and October will be enlivened by the companionship of flowers. No matter what degree of interest one normally has in wild flowers, few could fail to be moved by the Alps in bloom. The Engadine is especially rich in its varieties, for here lies the boundary between eastern and western alpine flora, and the great range in altitude, from one end of the valley to the other, and from valley floor to snowline, all contribute to an abundance of species.

This is not the place to describe all the plants one is likely to meet in these mountains. Those sufficiently interested in putting a name to the flowers are advised to consult one of the many handy books on the market that deal with them (see Appendix B). However, a word or two of a more general tone.

Alpine pastures are perhaps the richest areas for flowers, and the most intoxicating for fragrance. Among them will be found drifts of crocus almost before the last snows have melted from them; then soldanellas, cowslips, oxlips, spring gentians and orchids of many different varieties. There will be spring anemones, polygonums and violas, the great yellow gentian and alpenroses in unruly shrubberies, blazing with colour through the best of summer.

Primulas are found in pastures, on mountain ledges and even growing in rock crevices of overhanging cliffs. In the Engadine I've found them shining bright from a bed of minute azaleas at 2,000 metres, and strung in a rock face at only 1,500 metres. Similarly there are the creamy stars of edelweiss peeping from grassy meadows, and also clinging to raw cliffs deep in shade.

Daphnes are found throughout the region; either the woody daphne mezereum, highly scented when in flower, or the low cluster of daphne cneorum, a sparkle of crimson amid the short grass. There are auriculas, saxifrages and androsace. There will be found the delicate bells of one or two campanulas and various fleshy sempervivums. But wherever you wander in these mountains and valleys, keep an eye open for a sudden wink of colour; the flowers will add so much to your day.

Many of the plants are protected by law. A list is published by the Cantonal authorities, and quite often illustrated posters of these flowers are seen displayed in railway stations, hotels and Post Offices. There are also Plant Protection Zones scattered throughout the valley where the picking of flowers is strictly forbidden. So please, walk in the valleys and mountains and be inspired by the plants you see. Study them, photograph them, breathe their heady perfume. But leave them for others to enjoy too.

Weather

In summer the weather pattern of the Engadine and Bregaglia tends to be rather more settled than experienced in some of the larger regions of the Western Alps. One feature worth noting in the Upper Engadine, however, is the tendency towards strong southerly winds during the afternoon. These will be especially felt in the lake region stretching from Maloja to St. Moritz where the valley is broad and open. These winds can be keen and quite cool, but appear to be a sign of settled weather in the Bregaglia.

Spring arrives at different times in various parts of the valley, depending upon altitude and position. Generally speaking, though, May is not a good month to visit, and June is the earliest to contemplate a walking trip there. Even then snow will be lying quite low and some of the walks described here will not be possible to tackle until July. But in June the weather is beginning to build its promise, the valley meadows are bright with flowers and the mountains are gleaming and fresh-looking. A lovely month, so long as you do not plan to cross any high passes.

Being a low valley under the influence of Italian weather patterns, the Bregaglia is often in better condition for 'high' walks earlier than anywhere in the Engadine.

July and August are of course high season months when the weather should be bright and warm for lengthy periods, although temperatures are a little lower than, say, in the Valais. But August can sometimes be damp, and as in most high mountain regions of the Alps, snow can fall at any time of the year. Since the Engadine in its upper levels lies at an altitude of around 1,800 metres, rainfall can quite easily turn to snow, even in August. Rainfall statistics for the Engadine show much lower figures than those for the Oberland, but higher than for the Valais.

In certain respects September is a better month; more settled and calm. Snow cover will be higher than at any other time in the summer, and from personal experience, tends to enjoy prolonged spells of fine weather, although in the Bregaglia autumnal mists can sometimes linger late into the morning. Nights will be turning cold and frosts should be expected. October, if settled, can be a truly magical month when the larch forests are a-dazzle with gold and walking through the crisp valleys is like stepping in dreams.

Notes for Walkers
It is hoped that this book will be used by casual walkers who may never have wandered an alpine valley before, as well as by the more experienced mountain wanderer aiming for the snowline. There is something here for everyone, and having spent many happy days ambling gently through low valleys in the company of wife and young children, as well as scrambling among the higher peaks, I am convinced that every level has its own spice, its own very special charm. Much of the pleasure of rambling in the Alps comes from the enormous variety of scenery that the paths lead through. That variety can be experienced to some degree even in the lowliest valley as well as upon the upper hillsides among the boundaries of heaven and earth. If the wanderer sets out with an eye for the views, for the flowers and shrubs and lichen-painted rocks in the meadows, for the streams and tarns and forests, he will never be disappointed with his day. However, the more adventurous the chosen route, the more prepared one must be for it. It is to be hoped, then, that the following few notes will be helpful towards that preparation, so to enable you to make the most of your holiday.

First of all, of course, the fitter you are upon arrival, the more likely you are to enjoy your walks to the full. The day you enter the Engadine Valley is not the day to start thinking about getting fit. Most ramblers will understand this and will have been taking walks at home before the holiday, so to avoid aching legs and a pounding heart from tackling a strenuous outing without first getting the body and limbs into shape. It is also worth remembering that even the valley bed of the Upper Engadine lies at a height of almost one and a half times that of Ben Nevis, and there are those who need time to adjust to the altitude. Don't make the mistake of taking on too much for the first day or so, but instead build up distance and height-gain steadily, day by day. Hopefully there will be found sufficient outings in this guide to enable most walkers to enjoy a good day out at any level. Every valley, hillside and ridge has its own unique flavour to sample at will.

The next point to consider is that of equipment, the choice of which can make or mar a walking holiday. Boots, naturally, are of prime importance. They should be well-fitting and comfortable, and 'broken-in' before embracing the Alps. Nowadays there are many lightweight boots on the market that are a great improvement on the old-fashioned heavier type, once in common use, and these are in the main quite suitable for wandering in the Engadine. Whilst suspicions have been voiced in respect of their waterproof qualities, it should be borne in mind that alpine walking is not of the same nature as wandering in the British mountains where one spends much time squelching through boggy terrain. Most of the paths included in this book will be free from mud. There will be few streams to wade through and, in summer, few patches of melting snow. Wet feet should be no great problem. For low valley walks along beaten-earth paths, strong shoes should be adequate.

Shorts may well be fine for most summer walks in the valleys, but upon the hillsides and higher, breeches are normally worn. A sudden breeze at 2,500 or 3,000 metres can seem pretty cool, and the weather can quickly change from warm sunshine to strong winds and rain. At the very least a warm pullover should be worn or carried in the rucksack, even on what starts out to be a very warm day, and waterproof cagoule as minimum protection against rain. A windproof anorak is highly recommended in addition to the pullover and waterproofs. For those going high onto the mountains, it would be sensible to consider taking headwear and gloves against a sudden change in the weather. Sunglasses should be worn at all levels, for the alpine light is often dazzling, strong with ultra-violet rays even on cloudy days, but especially when reflected from a snowfield or glacier. Glacier cream or similar skin protection is advised to combat the burning rays of high altitude sun.

A small day sack should be sufficient to contain spare clothing and other necessary items such as first aid kit, map and compass, whistle, torch and spare batteries and water flask and food, on most of the outings except multi-day tours, on which overnight equipment will need to be carried.

A word about drinking water in the mountains. Most of the streams seen tumbling down the hillsides should be safe enough to drink from, unless sheep, goats or cows are grazing above. I have personally never had any problem from drinking directly from any mountain stream, but if in doubt it is suggested that you limit your drinking whilst on a walk, to those hewn-out log troughs found frequently in most valleys. These are filled from a gushing spring-fed pipe and will be pure enough for drinking. Water bottles should be topped up here too.

Finally, for those holiday makers who prefer to walk in the company of a group, several of the Engadine's tourist offices arrange day walks for visitors throughout the summer. Enquire at the information office of your particular village base for specific details. Most walks thus organised are guided free of charge to guests staying in the town or village in which they begin.

Paths and Waymarks

By far the majority of paths and tracks to be followed will be routes that have been used for centuries by farmers and chamois hunters going about their daily business; from alp to alp, or from one valley to the next by way of an ancient pass, or up onto a ridge where chamois might be spotted. A few have been made in comparatively recent times, either by the local commune or by the Swiss Footpath Protection Association *(Schweizerische Arbeitsgemeinschaft für Wanderweg)*, or by members of the SAC in order to reach a mountain hut.

Of the officially-maintained paths there are two varieties, both signposted and waymarked with paint flashes; the *Wanderweg* and *Bergweg*. A *Wanderweg* is a path that remains either in the valley itself, or runs along the hillside at a moderate altitude. They are well-maintained and graded at a much more gentle angle than the *Bergweg*. Along many of them a bench seat will have been provided at a particular vantage point. The paths are signposted with a white plate containing the name of the immediate locality and, often, the altitude; with finger posts painted yellow directing towards the next major landmark, be it a pass, lake or village. The estimated time allowed to reach this landmark will be indicated in minutes *(Min)* or hours (*Stunden* in German-speaking areas, *Ore* in Italian language localities). Along the trail occasionally yellow signs or paint flashes on rocks give reassurance that you are still on the correct route.

A *Bergweg* is a mountain path which ventures higher than that of a *Wanderweg*. These paths will generally be rougher, more narrow, sometimes fading if not in regular use. These are for walkers who should be properly equipped, for they lead to remote areas, often through very rugged terrain. Signposting is similar to that for a *Wanderweg*, except that the outer sections of the finger posts will be painted red and white, and paint flashes along the route will also be red and white. There may well be the occasional cairn to offer additional aid in certain areas where the path has faded away, and in the event of low cloud obscuring the onward route, it is essential to study the area of visibility with great care before venturing on to the next paint flash or stone cairn.

Safety in the Mountains

Without wishing to be alarmist or over-dramatic, it is the duty of the guidebook writer to draw attention to the dangers that do exist in mountain regions. A sudden storm, stones dislodged from above, a twisted ankle on a scree slope etc., each of which could cause problems if the party is not prepared to cope with the emergency.

Wandering along a valley path should be harmless enough, but the higher one ventures in the mountains the more realistic the walker's approach should be. Walk carefully, be properly equipped, take local advice as to the weather prospects and plan your day accordingly. Take care not to dislodge stones from the path, for they may well fall onto an unwary walker, farmer or animal some way below. Never be too proud to turn back should you find the route takes longer than you'd thought, or if the way becomes difficult or dangerous. Watch for signs of deteriorating weather and study well the map in conjunction with your compass before visibility is reduced. Think ahead.

In the unhappy event of an accident, stay calm. Should the party be large enough to send for help - whilst someone remains behind with the injured member - make a careful note first of the exact location where the injured can be found. If there is a mountain hut nearby, seek assistance there. If a valley habitation is nearer, find a telephone and dial 01 47 47 47 for rescue services, *but only if absolutely essential.* essential.

The international distress call is a series of six signals (either blasts on a whistle, or flashes with a torch after dark) spaced evenly per minute, followed by one minute's pause, then repeat with a further six signals. The reply is three signals per minute, followed by a minute's pause.

Holiday insurance policies can often include mountain walking in the Alps, but check the small print for certain exclusion clauses. Specific mountain insurance cover is available for British citizens from specialist companies who often advertise in the U.K. climbing press. Remember, rescue services in Switzerland are extremely costly.

Glacier Crossing

Very few routes described within these pages venture on or near glaciers. However, a few do, so a word about glacier-crossing might be considered appropriate.

To the inexperienced, glaciers can be exceedingly dangerous places for the unprepared. Not only the ice itself, riven as it might be with deep crevasses, but the moraine walls on either side, and the glacial slabs immediately below. All should be treated with caution. Since it is assumed that walkers will not be equipped with ice axes, crampons or ropes, it should be stressed that on no account should you wander onto any glacier that is snow-covered. Should you have chosen a route that leads across one, and you find upon arrival that it is still so covered, either enquire at the nearest hut about the possibility of hiring a guide for the crossing, or return another way. However, should you come to a 'dry' glacier, that is to say, one that is free of snow cover, proceed with caution. Some glaciers in the mountains have trails crossing them, marked with paint flashes on rocks, or by cairns placed upon them, and you may proceed with a wary eye for any crevasses that must be avoided.

Moraine walls are composed of the broken rock and grit that have been spewed to one side by the moving ice. Some of these walls rise to gigantic proportions - above the Morteratsch Glacier, for example. But no matter how tempting they might be, be wary of climbing onto them except at specially marked places, for they can be unstable and dangerous.

Sometimes the route may lead below glaciers - that which leads between the Sasc Furä and Sciora huts in Val Bondasca is one such - and then you will be faced with crossing glacial slabs washed by the streams that flow from the icefield above. These slabs can be extremely slippery, so do take care. Watch out also for any stones that might come clattering down from above, brought by those streams. Move carefully but quickly to reach safe ground.

But to reiterate an earlier warning: Never be too proud to turn back. If you're unsure, and there's no-one near to hand with experience to help you over, return by an alternative path. The mountains are there to enjoy, not to be threatened by.

Grading of Walks

The walks in this book are designed to help you make the most of your holiday in the Engadine and adjacent valleys, and since it is hoped that walkers of all degrees of commitment will find something useful contained within, it seems that a grading system might be helpful in directing you to the standard of outing of particular interest to individual walkers. Since grading is not an exact science, the three categories I have chosen will necessarily cover a fairly wide spectrum.

Grade 1: Suitable for family outings. Mostly short distances will be involved along easy-graded paths or tracks with little change of height to contend with.

Grade 2: Moderate walking on mostly clear footpaths; some will be *Wanderweg* paths, others *Bergweg* trails with some altitude gains. Walkers should be adequately shod and equipped.

Grade 3: More strenuous routes on rough paths. Some scrambling may be involved. High passes to cross, some glacial involvement (individual routes will be so marked at specific headings) and possibly scree work. Steep ascents and descents, and fairly long distances involved. Those attempting these routes should be well equipped.

Recommended Maps

The *Landeskarte der Schweiz* series of maps that cover the Engadine and Bregaglia are magnificent works of art that breed excitement in the heart of any map enthusiast. Open any sheet and a picture of the country immediately leaps from the paper. By clever use of shading, contours and colouring, the line of ridges and rock faces, the flow of glaciers and streams, the curve of an amphitheatre, the narrow cut of a glen, the expanse of a lake and the forest cover of a hillside all announce themselves clearly. But which maps to use? What scale to choose?

It is to be hoped that the descriptions given in this book, together with the superb waymarking on the ground, will make it unnecessary to spend a fortune on maps. But at the head of each section a note is given as to the specific 1:50,000 sheets covering that area. Obviously the best detail will be found on the 1:25,000 series, but ten or more of these would be required to cover the regions included within these pages. Only six of the 1:50,000 would be needed for the same area. However, at a scale also of 1:50,000 Kümmerly and Frey have published one single sheet entitled 'Oberengadin' which is well worth trying to find. This *Wanderkarte* covers the Upper Engadine from Maloja to Cinuos-chel on one side, and the Bregaglia on the reverse, with an inset of the National Park area at a scale of 1:100,000. In addition, walking routes are drawn in red, and there's a summer and winter pictorial profile also included. This is exceptional value and, at the time of writing, could be purchased from several book stores in the Engadine.

For a good general picture of the region, *Landeskarte der Schweiz*

1:100,000 sheets, numbers 44, 'Maloja Pass' and 39, 'Flüela Pass' are very useful and excellent value. Again, details of sheets are given at the head of each section.

Using the Guide

A brief word of explanation about this guide. Distances are given throughout in kilometres and metres, as are heights. These details are taken directly from the map and are so chosen to avoid confusion when referring to the map one moment, and to the book the next. Times are given for each of the walks and are approximate only. They make no allowance for rest stops or photographic interruptions. Naturally they will invariably be found slow by some walkers, fast for others. I make no apology for this; they are given as a rough guide only. My suggestion is that you compare your walking speed with that proposed by this book, and either add to, or subtract from, for future outings. Remember, though, these routes are designed not for racing, but for a simple enjoyment of fine mountain scenery.

In descriptions of routes, directions 'left' and 'right' are used to apply to the direction of travel, whether in ascent, descent or traverse. However, when used in reference to the banks of glaciers or streams, 'left' and 'right' indicate the direction of flow, ie: looking downwards. Where doubts might occur a compass direction is also given.

A note too, on the use of the word 'alp'. Commonly the Alps are taken to mean the chain of mountains spreading in an arc from the Mediterranean to the Julians of Yugoslavia. However, traditionally, 'alps' were to the mountain peasants, not the peaks themselves, but those high pastures on which cattle were taken to graze during the summer months. Many of the walks in this guide wander through 'alp' hamlets, linking the high pastures with all their lush fragrance and idyllic views. They are indeed, alps among the Alps.

Finally, I have made every effort to check these routes for accuracy and it is to the best of my belief that the guide goes into print with all details correct. However, changes are made from time to time; paths may be re-routed, certain landmarks altered. Any corrections necessary to keep the book up-to-date will be made in future printings wherever possible. Should you find any changes that are required, I'd very much appreciate a brief note of the particular route and alteration. Correspondence on this via the publisher would be gratefully received.

Piz Badile from Val Bondasca

Alp Tombal, with Sciora peaks in the background

Val Bregaglia

VAL BREGAGLIA

Lej dal Lunghin

UPPER ENGADINE

Piz Lunghin

MALOJA

CASACCIA

Lägh da Cavloc

Val Forno

Piz de la Margna

Piz Muretto

Monte del Forno

Cap. da l'Albigna

Cap. del Forno

Forno Glacier

Val Albigna

Cima di Castello

Monte Sissone

Albigna Glacier

N

SCALE

0   5 kms

The Bregaglia (or Bergell) is the smallest of the southern valleys of the Canton of Graübunden leading down into Italy by a series of natural terraces from the saddle of the Maloja Pass. As you descend the countless hairpins from the broad lakes and snowy peaks of the Upper Engadine, you are clearly entering a very different world. The Bregaglia is low, narrow, steep-walled, washed with the warm breath of Italy, lit by a soft and lucid light. Down there the villages may have the neat orderliness of Switzerland, but the architecture is distinctly Italian, with Italian names in the streets and Italian voices in the shops and surrounding meadows. Breezes from Italy stir the leaves in the chestnut trees and bring with them the warm flavour of the Lombardy plains.

It doesn't feel like the Alps, but above rise magnificent peaks of granite with glaciers flowing from them, and from the glaciers come wild torrents in cascades of spray to water lush meadows and green woods below.

It's only twenty-three kilometres from the Maloja Pass to the Italian border at Castasegna, but there's a difference in altitude of more than eleven hundred metres, and a whole world of culture and pace and atmosphere. Bregaglia is a valley of gracious warmth and colour, of olde-worlde calm. You can sense it in the villages as you tread the rough cobbled streets and alleyways, and you can feel it on the hillsides where peasant farmers swing their scythes with that timeless rhythm that has been carried down through numberless generations of haymakers and goatherders. High on the green hillsides are perched tiny alp hamlets with their staggeringly beautiful views; hamlets of ancient stone-based, timber-walled chalets and haybarns, they belong to the mountainside as surely as do the angled pines and weathered boulders wearing lichen and moss jackets. Up there, on the northern slopes far far above the valley, is a wonderland of tree and shrub and flower and impossibly steep pasture broken now and then by a ribbon of stream, a brief levelling of meadow with a huddle of barns and chalets, and a traversing path unrivalled for its glorious panoramas. Across the unseen depths of the valley, where the woods of chestnut and beech and walnut grow, there rises a skyline formed by 'a coronet of domes and massive pinnacles carved out of grey rocks'. The peaks that head the Val Bondasca.

The southern wall of the Bregaglia rises mysterious from the forested darkness of its lower slopes. Hidden in this wall of mountain runs the Forno valley, a long ramp leading from eternal snows to grey moraine and green vale. Between Forno and Bregaglia comes the wild arctic savagery of the Albigna glen, but all you see of this from the valley is the huge wall of its dam blocking the secrets of the glen from the outside world. Then comes the finest of them all; the Val Bondasca which in turn is sliced by the shaft of the Trubinasca glen. 'He must be very dull of soul indeed who could not see without a catch of his breath the sudden upward surge of the Bondasca peaks of Badile and Cengalo.'

This then, is Val Bregaglia, and there's no better way to explore it than on foot, following the paths that lead step by step into a world of immense beauty and wonder.

Main Valley Bases:

Maloja (1,815m) is a straggling village well-situated for the exploration of the upper reaches of Val Bregaglia, especially for introductory walks into the Val Forno - and also for much of the Upper Engadine. It has hotels, a Youth Hostel in the main street, and a campsite. This is reached by way of a rough track leading from the main Engadine road at the southern end of the Lake of Sils. The campsite is a short distance along this, near the lakeside. In the village there are food shops, tourist information office and Post Office. Although a car would be helpful here, it is by no means essential on account of the frequent Postbus service down the Maloja Pass into the Bregaglia.

Vicosoprano (1,067m) is perhaps the best village centre in the Bregaglia proper, with some fine old houses, hotels, *pension* and a campsite that is very much a gathering ground for climbers, and found south of the village and separated from it by the bypass road. Good facilities and cheaper than Maloja. There are shops, bank and dairy in the village, and Post Office near the campsite.

Promontogno (821m) has a Youth Hostel (key and signing-in at *(Pension Sciora)* on a lane leading to the neighbouring village of Bondo in the mouth of Val Bondasca; also two *pensions* in the main street. A typical Bregaglia village with thick stone-walled houses leaning together across narrow cobbled streets, this makes a convenient base for walks into Val Bondasca and up to Soglio and beyond through the chestnut woods to the north-west.

Soglio (1,097m) must be one of the loveliest villages in all the Alps, with certainly one of the most dramatic views, looking as it does across the Bregaglia and into Val Bondasca with those jagged Scioras stabbing at its head. A small village reached by way of a narrow twisting road from Promontogno (Postbus from Promontogno Post Office, which is round at the western end of the village), it occupies a projecting shelf of hillside with pastures and haybarns all around. For accommodation Soglio has hotels and *pensions*. It has small grocery stores in the narrow streets - and a vision of splendour from every corner.

Mountain Huts:
Four huts serve the Bregaglia regions. Each is owned by the SAC, and each one is situated in the mountains walling the southern side of the valley. *Capanna del Forno* (2,574m) will be found above the east bank of the Forno Glacier. *Capanna da l'Albigna* (2,336m) is perched in wild terrain above the dammed Albigna lake, and separated from the Forno valley by a rough ridge breached by a convenient pass linking the two. The western ridge walling the Albigna glen has a brace of passes allowing access to *Capanna di Sciora* (2,117m). This hut occupies a ledge high above the Val Bondasca with the magnificent Sciora aiguilles rising immediately behind. This, in turn, is separated from *Capanna Sasc Furä* (1,904m) by a spur extending from the North East Ridge of Piz Badile.

Each of these huts is reached by at least one interesting route, given below, and their linking in a multi-day tour makes a very fine outing for experienced mountain walkers. Route descriptions for this tour are also outlined below.

VAL BREGAGLIA ROUTES

Route 1:   The Bregaglia Circuit

Grade:	3
Distance:	66 kilometres
Time:	6-7 days
Maps:	Landeskarte der Schweiz 1:50,000 series
	Nos.268 'Julier Pass' and 278 'Monte Disgrazia'
	Kümmerly and Frey 'Wanderkarte-Oberengadin'
	1:50,000

By linking a number of the routes detailed below, a magnificent high route circuit of the Bregaglia mountains can be achieved, thereby giving a challenge for experienced mountain trekkers with a week's holiday to spare. Depending upon the weather, fitness of the individual and condition of the passes, the circuit could be achieved in less than six days. But this is a long-distance outing to be wandered steadily. Find time to stop and study the flowers or views, the construction of an old haybarn, the flood of light into the valley below. The best time to attempt the circuit is between July and the end of September; preferably the later the better, when huts will be less crowded and you can have the paths more or less to yourself.

It is a challenging route and one that should not be taken too lightly. There are several high passes to be crossed, short stretches of glacier to negotiate, and some wild terrain. But throughout the views are enticing, ever-varied and alive with interest. First of all the northern wall of the Bregaglia is traversed from east to west, enjoying the superb panorama of jagged peaks opposite, the alp hamlets near at hand, and the deep shaft of the valley below. Then, after leaving Soglio, drop into the Bregaglia and ascend the lovely Val Bondasca, through the Trubinasca, then keeping high, traverse the southern glens and mountains, over glaciers and rough passes before descending through the Forno valley to Maloja.

Overnight stops will be made in the villages of Maloja, Casaccia and Soglio, and in SAC huts of Sasc Furä, Sciora, Albigna and Forno. Supplies may be bought in the villages, meals are normally available in the huts. An ice axe could be useful.

Begin the circuit in the Upper Engadine at Maloja, and take Route 5 over the Lunghin and Septimer passes to Casaccia in the Bregaglia near the foot of the Maloja Pass. Day two takes in the classic high route through Val Maroz, Val da Cam and the upper alp pastures of Plan Vest and Tombal to the wonderful village of Soglio (Route 8.) From Soglio, drop down through the chestnut woods to Promontogno where Route 17 will be taken up to the Sasc Furä hut. It would be feasible to continue over Colle Vial (Route 18) to the Sciora hut on the same day, but Sasc Furä occupies such a delectable site that it is recommended to spend some hours of relaxation there, and continue across to the Sciora hut the following day.

Again, it would be possible to link the stage from Sciora to Albigna (Route 19) with that from Albigna to Forno (Route 22), but each region has its own specific charm, its own atmosphere, that it would be better to spend a night at each. On leaving the Forno hut, take Route 4 in reverse down the glacier and long valley back to Maloja.

Individual details of each hut are given under the specific route descriptions notes.

VAL FORNO

Position: At the junction of Val Bregaglia and Upper Engadine, extending southward from Maloja.
Maps: Landeskarte der Schweiz 1:50,000 series
                No.268 'Julier Pass'
                1:100,000 series No.44 'Maloja Pass'
                Kümmerly and Frey 'Wanderkarte-Oberengadin'
                1:50,000
Valley Base: Maloja (1,815m)
Hut: Capanna del Forno (2,574m)

The Forno glen has three faces. As you wander into it from Maloja the first impression is one of a green and pleasant valley, gentle, bright with flowers and shrubs. There's a broad track, very popular in summer, that leads to the Cavloc tarn; a sparkling sheet of water in which is mirrored the reflection of Piz dei Rossi. South of the tarn the valley grows a little more wild. It forks at Plan Canin; south-east towards the Muretto Pass and Italy, south-west as the Val Forno proper.

Continuing into the Val Forno, one enters a desolate region of grey moraine boulders and rock, the milky glacial stream tumbling through from icefields out of sight. But nature is taking over now that the glaciers are receding, and in years to come this will be transformed into a wild garden. Flowers are already establishing themselves among the grit and rocks left by the distant glaciers. Wandering through this landscape of apparent lifelessness, the observant walker will begin to understand the power of nature's tireless industry and art.

Then the moraine wilderness is left behind and a third face of the Forno is shown. This is the snow and ice world of the Forno Glacier. Jutting peaklets rise from the snowfields, and thrusting bastions of

35

granite enclose the glacier in a great amphitheatre of considerable wild charm.

Route 2: Maloja (1,815m) - Lägh da Cavloc (Cavolocciosee) (1,907m)

Grade: 1
Distance: 3.5 kilometres
Height gain: 92 metres
Time: 1 hour

Although this is a very short walk, it makes an extremely pleasant outing. It's an easy track, gently graded, with shrubs growing in some profusion on either side, and trail-side cliffs here and there in which you'll see masses of pink primulas blooming early in the summer. Later, in September, bilberries are there in vast quantities among the trees.

The lake itself is a delightful spot, ideal for a picnic. On its south-eastern shore there's a restaurant overlooking the water, but the best views are to be had from the north-west where you gaze along the lake to the low alp buildings on the far side, and above the massed pines where rises the shapely peak of Piz dei Rossi (3,026m). A very pretty scene, popular with Engadine families as well as with visitors.

From the village street in Maloja follow the road towards the head of the Pass. (There are several unmade lay-bys for car parking.) At the first bend of the road a path branches off to the left. It leads through trees and comes to a group of houses and haybarns with a scoop of pastureland ahead. Follow the path down to the pastures and take the track that swings round to cross a bridge a little beyond a farm building. This track now winds its way among trees and shrubs and beside small cliffs. It leads all the way to Lägh da Cavloc.

Whilst the broad track leads to the far end of the tarn, passing the restaurant and heading towards Alp Cavloc, the recommendation is to strike away from it as soon as you come level with the tarn. There are signs of others having done this; a narrow path working to the right, skirting the water's edge and reaching the north-western end of the tarn where the views are lovely. The narrow path makes a circuit of the tarn and is highly recommended.

An alternative return route to Maloja leaves Lägh da Cavloc at its northern end on a path signposted to Lägh da Bitaburgh (1,854m), a much smaller tarn than Cavloc, overlooking the Val Bregaglia a short distance above Maloja Pass.

Lägh da Cavloc (Cavolocciosee) and Piz dei Rossi.

Route 3: Maloja (1,815m) - Muretto Pass (2,562m)

Grade: 3
Distance: 7 kilometres
Height gain: 747 metres
Time: 3-3½ hours

The Muretto Pass is an important saddle in the ridge linking the Bregaglia group of mountains with those of the Bernina massif, and forms an old trading route - used since the fourteenth century - from Maloja to Chiesa in the Italian Val Malenco. (8-9 hours away.) The path up to the pass is a little rough in places, but would make an interesting training walk. From the Italian side there are wonderful views across to Monte Disgrazia (3,678m), one of the most dramatic mountains in the region.

Follow Route 2 as far as Lägh da Cavloc. Continue along the main track to reach the long, low buildings of Alp da Cavloc and go beyond it on a narrower path among trees and then descending towards the valley bed. Along this path you pass a small hut on your right and soon after, come to a signpost directing the Muretto Pass trail left, away from the Forno Valley which here breaks away right into the moraine wilderness.

Glacial moraine, Forno valley

Go down to the stream and cross over on a small bridge. The path now works its way up-valley on the eastern side of the stream. For much of the year there is a long strip of snow coming down the bed of the valley from the snowfield cupped between Piz dei Rossi and Monte del Forno. The path avoids this by climbing above it to the left. As you gain height it becomes clear that there are two cols. The one to aim for is that on the left. On reaching the pass you stand on the frontier between Switzerland and Italy, and the border between the Bernina mountains to your left, and those of the Bregaglia to your right.

The descent to Maloja, by reversing the path of ascent, will occupy about two hours.

Route 4:   Maloja (1,815m) - Capanna del Forno (2,574m)

Grade: 3 (Rough walking, and a section of glacier to be
              crossed.)
Distance: 10 kilometres
Height gain: 759 metres
Time: 3½-4 hours

This walk to the Forno hut makes a fine introduction to the world of high mountains, and as you follow the path from Maloja, so you pace the transition from a world of soft meadows and lakes and woodlands, to one of arctic sterility. It's a walk with much to commend it, from so many angles. It's an education in mountain structure. It's a trail of botanic interest, and a walk of conflicting scenic pleasures.

The Forno hut itself has changed somewhat since it was built in 1889 as a private enterprise largely financed by Theodor Curtius (see Klucker's autobiography), but later presented to the Swiss Alpine Club. Nowadays it has room for 100 in its dormitories, and is open for the summer between July and the end of September with a guardian in residence. It also has a guardian in winter, too, and between times a section remains unlocked for off-season climbers. When the guardian is in residence there is a restaurant service, so walkers can make a day out with the possibility of refreshment at the hut.

Follow Route 3 as far as the signpost junction for the Muretto Pass trail. Take the main path as it bears right into the rough grey moraine valley towards the snout of the glacier some way ahead. The path becomes less well-defined, but red paint flashes direct the route along the right-hand side of the valley (the true left bank) to reach the Forno Glacier. (See notes on Glacier Crossing in Introductory section.) The route climbs onto the glacier, and as the angle eases towards the centre, bears leftwards (heading south-east) to gain the true right bank of the icefield. Following markers the trail gradually improves as it climbs into the cwm formed by ridges joining Monte del Forno with Monte Rosso. The hut is found among slabs of granite on the corner of a green terrace overlooking the Forno Glacier.

BREGAGLIA NORTH

Position:	Stretching from Maloja in the east, to the Italian frontier at Castasegna.
Maps:	Landeskarte der Schweiz 1:50,000 series No.268 'Julier Pass' 1:100,000 series No.44 'Maloja Pass' Kümmerly and Frey 'Wanderkarte-Oberengadin' 1:50,000
Valley Bases:	Maloja (1,815m), Casaccia (1,458m), Vicosoprano (1,067m), Promontogno (821m), Soglio (1,097m)

This northern wall of the Val Bregaglia has paths winding along it that present some of the most spectacular walking in all the Alps. It's a green and lush series of hillsides with woods and pasture terraces, alp

View to Piz Corvatsch from path to Lunghin Pass

chalets and haybarns. Above the high pastures rise grey mountain tops with dipping ridges through which accessible passes lead to or from hidden hanging valleys. By using these passes one can branch out on long walks heading for far-off villages and quiet corners of other mountains. But best of all are the panoramas south from the high alp hamlets; views across the depths of the valley into the Albigna and Bondasca glens; views that catch your breath with wonder and exhilaration and stay alive in memory long after your return home.

**Route 5:   Maloja (1,815m) - Lunghin Pass (2,645m) -
             Septimer Pass (2,310m) - Casaccia (1,458m)**

Grade: 2
Distance: 13 kilometres
Height gain: 830 metres   Height loss: 1,187metres
Time: 5½ hours

By walking from Maloja to Casaccia an interesting link may be made between the Upper Engadine and Val Bregaglia proper. It begins with bright views of Upper Engadine lakes and snow peaks, and ends with a sudden open view of the Bregaglia running away before you. In

40

between the two there is much wild country; historic, geographically important country with the possibility of sighting marmots or chamois along the way. Since Postbuses run frequently over the Maloja Pass, it is feasible to return to Maloja from the little village of Casaccia at the conclusion of the walk.

The path begins some 200 metres north of Maloja Post Office, on the road leading towards Silvaplana. It climbs away from the road opposite a house named Chesa Irene, and is signposted to Pass dal Lunghin. It's a narrow, steeply climbing path at first that soon reaches a track before returning to footpath once more. Where alternative paths branch away, a clear signpost points in the right direction. After a short while a rather fine view opens across the Engadine, with the blue expanse of the Lake of Sils below, and the snowy crown of Piz Corvatsch rising over all.

Eventually you come above the treeline on a rough path marked with regular paint flashes, and about two hours from Maloja it brings you into a desolate bowl of scree and boulder in which nestles the chilly-looking Lägh dal Lunghin; birthplace of the River Inn which gives the Engadine its name. The path goes round the left-hand side of the tarn and climbs then up to the obvious saddle of Pass dal Lunghin some 160 metres higher and marked with a metal signpost announcing the watershed. From this raw little saddle the Inn eases down into the Engadine and flows by a devious route to the Black Sea. On the other side flows a meagre brook, unseen from the pass, to become the Maira, which flows out to the Adriatic, and to the north-west flows another, which in turn joins several larger streams to become the Rhine. This, of course, empties into the North Sea.

Between the Lunghin and Septimer passes lies a scene of barren rocks and empty mountains and a long slither of sad pasture easing off to the north. The path leads among rough rocks leftwards round the head of this sorry valley for about 40 minutes to meet a broader track coming from the right. (The village of Bivio lies at the foot of this track, below the Julier Pass.) As you wander along this path to the Septimer Pass, keep an eye and an ear open for marmots and chamois. The path and the track meet at the Pass itself, about three and a half hours from Maloja.

Cross the Pass heading left into a tight valley to pass a couple of neat buildings and stables. The path narrows, crosses to the left bank of the stream and begins to lose height quickly. Some very steep zig-zags bring you down to the junction of a broader valley, Val Maroz, at 1,799 metres. Remaining on the left bank of the stream the path continues down, with the Val Bregaglia coming into view. More zig-zags, but less steep this time, eventually lead into the village of Casaccia. (Hotels here, and Postbus connections for Maloja.)

Route 6: Casaccia (1,458m) - Val Maroz - Septimer Pass (2,310m) - Bivio (1,769m)

Grade:	2
Distance:	12 kilometres
Height gain:	852 metres Height loss: 541 metres
Time:	4½-5 hours

An interesting day's walking on a straightforward path which follows an ancient trading route. It's a steep haul up to the Septimer Pass from Casaccia, but a long and gradual descent on the far side takes you down to the village of Bivio. This could make a pleasant initial stage of a departure for home, followed by Postbus journey to Chur from Bivio. Alternatively, a return to the Engadine and Bregaglia can be achieved also by Postbus over the Julier Pass.

The path begins in Casaccia at the southern end of the main street, and climbs in a long sweep to the right before heading up into the Val Maroz behind the village. After an hour's walking you come to the alp buildings of Maroz Dora on the opposite side of the rushing stream. Shortly after this the way forks; left to cross the stream and delve deeper into Val Maroz, and right to climb steeply into the narrow defile down which dashes the stream from the Septimer Pass. Take the right fork and follow this narrow zig-zag path all the way to the Pass, which is reached in about 2¾ hours from Casaccia.

At the Septimer Pass the track is clear as it slants off directly ahead. Ignore alternatives to right and left. The way leads through the sweep of valley. In its lower reaches a number of side streams join the main river, and here the way can sometimes be a little damp. A kilometre or so above Bivio the track leaves the stream's company and cuts off to the north-west to enter the village in its main street. (Bivio is a pleasant village with three hotels, grocery store and Post Office.)

Route 7: Casaccia (1,458) - Septimer Pass (2,310m) - Forcellina Pass (2,672m) - Juf (2,126m)

Grade:	3
Distance:	13 kilometres
Height gain:	1,214 metres Height loss: 546 metres
Time:	6½ hours

A rather strenuous walk, this route crosses some wild country around the Forcellina Pass before descending to the Jufer Alp of the Aversthal, and reaching the highest village in Switzerland to be inhabited all-year round. Juf (sometimes known as Avers-Juf) has *pension* and Youth Hostel accommodation.

Follow Route 6 as far as the Septimer Pass, where you bear left and trace a path up to the saddle found to the north of Piz Forcellina. Once over this saddle the way swings right above a little tarn and skirts the rocky slopes to a point a little below Fuorcla da la Valletta. Here the route zig-zags down leftwards to enter the valley of the Jufer Rhine, the Aversthal, eventually to reach the little village of Juf.

To make a multi-day circuit, wander the six kilometres down-valley next day as far as Avers-Cresta (1,959m) using this as a 'rest day', then on the third day continue down to the next village of Cröt, where you then turn south into the Madriserthal. After about 8 or 9 kilometres of walking through this valley, it divides. Take Val Prassignola, the eastern (left-hand) valley, and climb this for two hours to reach the Forcella di Prassignola (2,724m) by way of a well-made path. There is another path dropping steeply from this pass, and leading through woods and meadows to Soglio.

Route 8:   Casaccia (1,458m) - Val Maroz - Val da Cam (2,433m) - Soglio (1,097m)

Grade: 2
Distance: 16 kilometres
Height gain: 975 metres   Height loss: 1,336 metres
Time: 6½ hours

This outing is one of the classic 'middle-mountain' walks of Switzerland. A long day's walking, certainly, but it is full of interest and variety. Keep your camera handy to capture some truly spectacular panoramas.

Follow Route 6 out of Casaccia and into the Val Maroz for the first hour, to reach the alp buildings of Maroz Dora on the other side of the stream. Shortly after this the way divides. Head left, cross the stream and enter the main stretch of Val Maroz on a broad track. This soon deteriorates to become little more than a faint path with paint flashes. It leads deeper into the valley, climbing through wild rock gardens of shrubs, juniper sprays and numerous cushion plants. There are alpenroses and daphne mezereum in a very colourful stretch, and the mountains rising all around to contain the views.

The southern wall of Val Bregaglia, from Tombal

Two hours from Casaccia another alp, Maroz Dent (2,035m) is reached. Here there's a little alp dwelling and a long cattle byre in a lovely setting. Beside it, a pentagonal walled sheepfold; below to the left, the rushing stream. The path drops down to the stream and crosses by way of a wooden bridge. Again the way divides; right, one trail goes farther up-valley to reach the Val da la Duana, and by way of a pass at its head drops down to join our route again some way above Soglio (Route 9); left, a narrow climbing path winds up the steep hillside ahead. This is our route.

Actually, there are two alternative paths here that join together a little below the false saddle that allows access to Val da Cam. One, an easier-graded trail, goes to the left of the stream tumbling down the hillside, while the other heads steeply on a narrow path to the right of the stream. Choose either alternative. Both are led by paint flashes up the hillside. At the head of the ascent a saddle is reached, guarded by a curious 'family' of lofty cairns. Beyond lie the pastures of Val da Cam. Wander through this gentle valley keeping more or less to the centre of it, and climb a grassy step at the far end. This brings you to the next level of the valley with the continuing path winding among the hillocks that obscure the pass through which one gains the hillside above Val Bregaglia.

Once through the strange rocky gateway of Pass da Cam, the Bregaglia begins to open out and displays its undisputed charm. The path loses height, then heads off to the right (westwards) on a descending traverse way above the valley. On the far side the mountains rise magnificently, dragging your eyes away from the narrow path along which you step. You come to a water trough constructed out of huge slabs of stone. Below stands the isolated farmstead of Plan Lo, but the path continues westward, loses itself among the boulders, but is then found again with a prominent marker post directing the route along the hillside.

Sometimes the path is extremely narrow and with a substantial drop to one side. Now and again it climbs over a bluff, sometimes it loses height; mostly it makes its steady traverse among a wild vegetation. Cadrin is a deserted alp with decaying buildings. Just beyond this, the path from Val da la Duana comes down to meet ours. The next alp is Lobbia; a meagre collection of dwellings and barns with a stream nearby: but the best of all is Plan Vest with its staggering view of the Sciora aiguilles, Cengalo and Piz Badile soaring into the heavens on the far side of the valley. Plan Vest is a string of fine alp chalets and haybarns tucked tightly against the steep hillside with a sloping apron of pasture before it. The continuing path crosses this pasture and drops down through the pine forest on a steep zig-zag of a path, separating Plan Vest from Tombal. Tombal is yet another alp with fabulous views and an air of magic about it. The path heads south past ancient buildings and across the pasture, then swings right and drops in a long and tiring descent all the way to Soglio.

As has already been mentioned, Soglio is one of the loveliest villages in all the Alps. It has hotel and *pension* accommodation, grocery stores, and Postbus link with the Val Bregaglia below.

**Route 9:   Casaccia (1,458m) - Val Maroz - Val da la Duana -
            Pass da la Duana (2,694m) - Soglio (1,097m)**

Grade: 2
Distance: 16 kilometres
Height gain: 1,236 metres   Height loss: 1,597 metres
Time: 8 hours

An alternative high route to Soglio, this is a deviation of Route 8 above. Follow Route 8 as far as the bridge crossing the Maroz stream below the alp buildings of Maroz Dent, then continue up-valley on a marked trail leading to the Val da la Duana. The path goes through this valley and over Pass da la Duana to gain the upper hillsides of the north wall of the Bregaglia above Cadrin alp. Once at Cadrin join Route 8 as far as Soglio.

Route 10: Casaccia (1,458m) - Roticcio (1,268m) - Durbegia (1,410m) - Soglio (1,097m)

Grade:	1 (A long walk, but on mostly clear and easily graded paths.)
Distance:	14 kilometres
Height gain:	142 metres Height loss: 503 metres
Time:	5 hours

Another Bregaglia classic, this route is locally known as the *Sentiero panoramico;* or in German, *Panoramahöhenweg.* It's not a high route in the sense that the two previously described walks are, but it offers similar views across to the peaks walling the valley to the south, albeit not with quite the same degree of drama as in Route 8, for example. But this walk also links villages and alp hamlets, wanders through pastures on a traversing series of paths, well-marked and with delight-ful features to study along the way. It *is* a long walk. Five hours of wandering, plus time to stop for a picnic, to rest, to photograph; but it is worth giving a day of a holiday to such an outing. For those who might consider it a little too long - perhaps with young families - I would suggest breaking the walk into two day-outings; the first from Casaccia to Parlongh, then descend to the valley by way of a path which leads through Muntac and Coltura to Stampa (Postbus along Val Bregaglia from here); the second stage from Stampa to Soglio via Caccior as described in Route 13 below.

La Panoramico leaves Casaccia at its southern (down-valley) end and heads along the valley, crosses the Maira river to its right bank and skirts the forest along the valley bed to a short distance before the village of Roticcio. The river has been busy in cutting the valley floor deeper below, while Roticcio stands some way above it with Val Furcella shafting behind. Roticcio is about one hour's walk from Casaccia. Thereafter the path continues in a south-westerly direction along the hillside with the valley now falling steadily deeper below, the route gaining height for a further hour until you reach the alp hamlet of Durbegia in its delightful setting. Beyond Durbegia the path still rises, cutting through forest, over a tumbling stream and round a spur of mountainside before beginning the long sloping traverse to Parlongh (1,274m) where an alternative path branches off to the left, allowing those who wish to break the route, to drop down to the valley at Stampa.

Our route, however, continues around the hillside with the views growing ever-more spectacular as a sudden bend in the path reveals before you a vista of enchantment. The final length of footpath that leads round the jutting spur of mountain beyond which Soglio lies, is a constant delight as Val Bondasca stretches away in all its splendour ahead.

Route 11: Vicosoprano (1,067m) - Roticcio (1,268m) - Val Furcela (2,369m) - Val Maroz - Casaccia (1,458m)

Grade: 2
Distance: 12 kilometres
Height gain: 1,302 metres   Height loss: 911 metres
Time: 6-6½ hours

A stiff climb, this outing ascends the northern wall of Val Bregaglia, and descends again by way of the Val Maroz to Casaccia. To find the start of the route, walk up-valley from Vicosoprano along the straight main road (not the bypass road that carries valley traffic), then cut off left across the meadows on a marked path which then crosses the river and heads up to the village of Roticcio. From there, it climbs north into the wedge of Val Furcela, and at its head, crosses into the Val da Cam a short distance from the saddle where a 'family' of lofty, slender cairns marks the way down into Val Maroz by a steep twisting path. Once in the bed of Val Maroz, cross the stream and follow the path beyond the alp buildings of Maroz Dent and continue down-valley all the way to Casaccia.

Route 12: Vicosoprano (1,067m) - Borgonovo (1,048m) - Stampa (994m)

Grade: 1
Distance: 4 kilometres
Height loss: 73 metres
Time: 1 hour

There are two routes linking these three villages, both of which are gentle undemanding strolls; perhaps ideal for a summer evening when shadows are long and the air is balmy and crickets buzzing in the grass.

One path leads over the river from Vicosoprano, then heads along the right bank downstream as far as Coltura, before doubling back down to the stone bridge at Stampa. The other keeps on the left side of the valley and wanders through the edge of the forest. Perhaps a round trip could be made by going down-valley one way, and returning by the other.

Route 13:   Stampa (994m) - Coltura (999m) - Soglio (1,097m)

Grade: 1
Distance: 4.5 kilometres
Height gain: 103 metres
Time: 1½ hours

This may well be a short stroll, but it has considerable charm and is a minor classic in its own right. It could be enjoyed as a morning's amble, with lunch in Soglio and the afternoon spent exploring the alleys and cobbled streets of this lovely village. The Postbus winds down into the valley from Soglio to join the main Postbus route for those who prefer this as a one-way walk. But for those who care to walk down again, there is another path through the chestnut woods to Promontogno. Or, as another option, link this walk with Route 14 below, steeply up to the alp Tombal for even more dramatic views.

Stampa lies roughly halfway between Borgonovo and Promontogno in Val Bregaglia. An attractive village, it has hotel and *pension* accommodation; and in *Ciasa Granda*, a fine 16th century house in the main street, there is now a museum devoted to the valley's unique history and culture. Stampa, incidentally, was home to the painter and sculptor, Alberto Giacometti, who died in 1966.

The path begins in the main street and is signposted to Soglio. It crosses the river on an old stone bridge and soon after reaches the little village of Coltura, noted for its curious piece of architecture, the so-called 'castle' of Castelmur. From Coltura the way gently wanders across the hillside to reach the hamlet of Caccior (933m), then steadily rises to Soglio's own terrace perch. An easy, gentle, lovely walk.

Route 14:   Soglio (1,097m) - Tombal (1,537m)

Grade: 2
Distance: 2 kilometres
Height gain: 440 metres
Time: 1¼ hours

Soglio

Tombal is such a magical place, perched as it is on a brief grassy shelf high above the Bregaglia, and with such delightful views, that it is well worth making the effort to walk up the extremely steep path from Soglio to discover it. There are no refreshments available there, nor streams from which to drink; so take a picnic lunch and a flask and enjoy hours of relaxation on the lip of the world, with a panorama spread before you that you're not likely to forget in a hurry.

From the cobbled square in front of the old hotel in Soglio, head left along the narrow street, then right into an alleyway with a sign directing to several different destinations; 'Cadrin-Val da Cam-Casaccia', 'Pass Duan-Val Maroz' etc. Tombal as such does not appear on direction posts until a little higher above the village.

The path through the alleyway leads between low stone walls, gaining height above the village to reach a road. Go up the road a few paces, then branch away from it to the right on another path that climbs steeply up the hillside between trees. Continue to follow this path all the way, in and out of trees, always steep and narrow, until suddenly you top a bluff, the trees having given way to an open space, and you realise you've entered another world. There is a haybarn, and a little pool of water just beyond it to capture reflections - and those magnificent views to the Scioras and Piz Badile way across the valley.

Bear left here and wander across the rolling pastureland to find Tombal proper; a line of photogenic old stone and timber buildings tucked tightly against the wooded hillside. They gaze out at a vision of unmarked splendour.

Route 15:   Soglio (1,097m) - Castasegna (688m)

Grade:	1
Distance:	4 kilometres
Height loss:	409 metres
Time:	1 hour

This is a gentle pastureland walk, especially fine in autumn when the colours of the beechwoods and chestnut trees are at their best, and when the first snows have dusted the Bondasca peaks opposite. It is a walk that embraces the tranquility of alpine pastoral life; the shorn meadows, the gurgling streams, the sweet-smelling haybarns. In spring the meadows are bright with flowers, the streams charged with melting snow. In summer there will be farmers scything the grass or raking the meadows for hay, cowbells ringing or goats bleating. In autumn the pastures are smooth and all-but deserted; perhaps farmers will be spreading manure to put back some goodness for next year's hay crop.

It's a walk that could be used as an extension of *La Panoramico* (Route 10), to complete the traverse of the Bregaglia, or as an outing in its own right. Take a Postbus to Soglio, spend time wandering the streets there, and then stroll down to Castasegna by this delightful path. An easy half-day, but no less satisfying for all that.

There are several paths bound for Castasegna from Soglio, but our route leads across the meadowlands west of the village, maintaining a fairly regular altitude for about two kilometres, before it turns sharply left and drops down round the edge of a minor band of rocks to wind its way to the valley bed at Castasegna on the Italian border.

VAL BONDASCA

Position:	At the western end of the Val Bregaglia and cutting south-eastwards from the main valley behind the villages of Promontogno and Bondo.
Maps:	Landeskarte der Schweiz 1:50,000 series No.278 'Monte Disgrazia' 1:100,000 series No.44 'Maloja Pass' Kümmerley and Frey 'Wanderkarte-Oberengadin'

1:50,000

Valley Bases: Promontogno (821m), Bondo (823m),
             Vicosoprano (1,067m)
Huts: Capanna Sasc Furä (1,904m),
             Capanna di Sciora (2,118m)

Without doubt the Val Bondasca is the loveliest, most dramatic of the side glens feeding into the Bregaglia. A small valley that rises steeply from warm pastures to a bold savagery of granite spires and glacial writhings, as you wander into it so you pass from an almost subtropical vegetation where there are ferns as high as a man's shoulders, to a world of lichen and minute rock plants and bare slabs.

Thick woods clothe the slopes that mask the valley's mouth. Here Bondasca is narrow and steep-walled and dark with shadow, but as you explore deeper into its recesses, so the valley begins to open out to reveal some of its splendours. On the right slices the mysterious Trubinasca glen, but above, the Bondasca spreads wide its welcome with one of the most enchanting cirques imaginable. Bounded by the huge walls of Cengalo and Badile on one side, and the craggy Cacciabella ridge on the other, rise the 'flamelike outlines of the fantastic Sciora peaks'; Sciora di Fuori, Punta Pioda, Ago di Sciora, Sciora Dadent. Wonderful peaks, they are, sharp as the blade of a knife, smooth-walled and a great temptation to rock climbers. From the walker's point of view they form a backcloth to dreams and the horizon within which days of pleasure are spent.

Route 16: Promontogno (821m) - Val Bondasca - Sciora Hut (2,118m)

Grade: 2
Distance: 6.5 kilometres
Height gain: 1,297 metres
Time: 4 hours

The Sciora Hut (Capanna di Sciora) occupies a shelf of rock among the steep moraines that lie immediately below the Sciora peaks, and looks out over the length of the Bondasca valley to the hillsides where sit Soglio, Tombal and Plan Vest. It is a splendid perch for a splendid hut. With room for 50, meals and drinks available, and with those lovely views over such contrasting scenery, it makes a natural point to aim for on a walk through the valley. But it is a very steep walk, too, so be prepared for a tiring day's exercise.

Opposite *Pension Sciora* in Promontogno's main road, a narrow cobbled street cuts back towards Bondo. The Youth Hostel will be

Sasc Furä Hut, Trubinasca Cirque

found along here on the left, and shortly after passing this you come to
a stone bridge over the river that comes pouring from the Bondasca
glen. (Across the bridge lies Bondo.) Immediately before this bridge a
path climbs up to the left. This is the start to our walk. It heads up
through trees, climbing quite steeply, and comes onto a track. This
drivable track heads along the Val Bondasca for some way, and by
driving along it from Bondo, an hour's walking time could be saved.
Follow the track to its end.

From the end of the track a clear path continues, but after a while
this divides. Take the left fork, which in effect continues in more or
less the same direction. (On the right the alternative path crosses the
river and climbs up to the Sasc Furä hut.) Along the main valley path
you come to the rough tangle of Alp Laret (1,368m) after about an
hour and a half from Promontogno. Around and beyond this alp there
are wild raspberries to tempt you towards the end of summer. Beyond
Alp Laret the way winds among boulders and a straggling vegetation,
but there is no difficulty in finding the route, for it is well-trodden and
waymarked with paint flashes at convenient points.

The route steepens and the path zig-zags among rocks and up a little
gully, and then finally works its way up the moraine wall to its crest
where the hut will be found.

Route 17: Promontogno (821m) - Sasc Furä Hut (1,904m)

Grade: 2
Distance: 6 kilometres
Height gain: 1,083 metres
Time: 3½ hours

The path to Sasc Furä is a magical one. It is also excessively steep and
taxing. In places footholds have actually been cut into the trunks of
trees in order to facilitate ascent. But upon emerging in a little
mountain glade where the Capanna Sasc Furä gazes out at a
wonderland of immense beauty, with a backing of great rock walls and
cascading glaciers, the walker knows without a glimmer of doubt that
he has arrived at a rather special belvedere.

The hut itself, owned by the Swiss Alpine Club, has sleeping
accommodation for 40, meals and drinks available, and is wardened
from the beginning of July until September.

Take Route 16 above as far as the path division a little beyond the
end of the motorable track in Val Bondasca. Where the path forks,
head right and cross the river on a wooden bridge. From the south
side of the river a faint path leads across a little rough meadow and
into thick vegetation (raspberries again) before beginning to climb
steeply. It is marked with paint flashes and occasional cairns, but on
the ground the path becomes more evident as you gain height.

The way continues, steeply, abruptly. A path not for the faint-
hearted, it remains among trees for much of the way and has only a
short spell when the gradient levels on a brief traverse right, across a
tumbling stream and among lofty pines, but then turns the edge of the
promontory up which the way lies, and climbs once more. Shortly
after this you suddenly come out of the shade of trees, emerge over a
bluff, and there stands the hut with Piz Badile's north ridge soaring
overhead. A most dramatic spot.

**Route 18: Sasc Furä Hut (1,904m) - Colle Vial (2,200m) -
Sciora Hut (2,118m)**

Grade: 3 (Some glacier crossing involved.)
Distance: 4 kilometres
Height gain: 296 metres   Height loss:82 metres
Time: 3½ hours

A natural route linking the two Bondasca huts, this crosses the rocky
spur extending from Piz Badile's north ridge and drops to the glacial

The Sciora peaks at the head of Val Bondasca

debris fanning below Piz Cengalo. It is a route that should only be attempted in settled weather and by experienced mountain trekkers.

From the Sasc Furä hut climb the smooth slabs immediately behind it (paint flashes) and follow a vague trail of markers and occasional stretches of boot-printed footpath heading steeply south towards the ridge of Piz Badile. The way leads up rough granite boulders, once the few trees and shrubs have been left behind, keeping rather to the right of the spur. But after about thirty minutes, cairns lead the route up towards the crest, slightly leftwards. In three quarters of an hour you will come to Colle Vial (at about 2,200 metres); a notch in the granite crest, guarded by a cairn and adequate paint markings. The view down the eastern side is sobering, for it drops very steeply with a series of ledges to the rocks and moraine of the Cengalo Glacier. The Sciora hut can be seen as a blob of red upon the moraine mound in the east, with the fabulous jagged peaks like great granite fence posts behind it.

Descend with caution on a narrow gritty path at first, that soon turns to a ledge 'ladder' down which you climb with the wall of the ridge leaning towards you. It's an exposed descent, but safe enough when taken with care. At the foot of the wall cairns and paint flashes lead through a boulder field and up to a moraine cone where vegetation is taking over. Beyond this the route crosses a number of glacial slabs with streams running down them. Take great care when crossing these. More boulder wilderness; more moraine; more streams and then a short stretch of glacier - littered with stones and grit - has to be crossed. The route is marked throughout with either paint flashes or cairns, but could be difficult in low cloud, and caution should be exercised at all times.

The final approach to the Sciora hut is across more moraine with the magnificent Sciora needles piercing overhead.

Route 19:   Sciora Hut (2,118m) - Cacciabella Pass (2,897m) - Albigna Hut (2,336m)

Grade: 3
Distance: 6.5 kilometres
Height gain: 779 metres   Height loss: 561 metres
Time: 4½ hours

The crossing of the Cacciabella ridge is one that is often made in summer by climbers and mountain trekkers as a convenient route to the Albigna region. There are, in fact, two passes; one on either side of the rock tower of Piz Eravédar (2,934m), that have been used for centuries (at least 200 years) by chamois hunters. The route described here is that for the southern pass. A note of warning should be heeded, though, and that is to set off only in clear weather. Should the clouds come down some difficulty may be experienced in locating the correct path.

Outside the Sciora hut a rock has been painted with the route indicated in large letters. It leads over rough boulder slopes in a north-easterly direction before veering round to the east beyond a spur projecting from the ridge. Paint flashes and the occasional cairn lead the way to a snowfield, then rocks, and up to a snow couloir above which a ledge brings you to a point below the pass. A steep rocky pitch will bring you onto the pass after about three hours of ascent from the hut.

On the Albigna side you look onto the east ridge of Piz Eravédar a little to the north of the pass. This ridge has to be crossed, and this is achieved by descending a short gully and working then onto the ridge itself where a faint track leads down to a saddle. The route now traverses northward below the second Cacciabella pass, then heads north-east and crosses a wild region of rocks, snow and slabs, with the turmoil of the Albigna glen far below. Soon the path leads onto wide grassy slopes some way above the cold-looking waters of the dammed

Albigna lake, and with sufficient markings to lead you on, eventually brings you to the dam a little after having been joined by another path, this one from Passo Val della Neve above to the left.

Cross the wall of the dam, and on the eastern side follow the clear path heading round to the right (south-eastwards) up the boulder slopes and to the hut.

Details of the Albigna hut are given in the Albigna section that follows. For descent to Val Bregaglia from here, either return along the hut path to the head of the dam and take the cable-car down to Pranzaira, or follow Route 20 in reverse.

ALBIGNA

Position:	Midway along the Val Bregaglia between Val Bondasca and the Maloja Pass, cutting due south from the main valley.
Maps:	Landeskarte der Schweiz 1:50,000 series Nos.268 'Julier Pass' and 278 'Monte Disgrazia' 1:100,000 series No.44 'Maloja Pass' Kümmerley and Frey 'Wanderkarte-Oberengadin' 1:50,000
Valley Base:	Vicosoprano (1,067m)
Hut:	Capanna da l'Albigna (2,336m)

From the Val Bregaglia the full impact of the Albigna region is hidden by the huge wall of the dam which blocks the upper glen from view and spreads in an immense sheet of concrete from one natural rock wall to the other. Behind this dam lie the icy waters of the lake, caused by holding back the streams draining from glaciers draped from the peaks at the head of the valley. It's a rather bleak scene when compared with that of Bondasca, by virtue of its minimal vegetation. However, the peaks jutting from the containing ridges are fine enough, and there are snowfields and glaciers a-plenty to contrast the lush greenery of Val Bregaglia. Under a less-than-perfect sky it appears to be an area of arctic desolation. But in that there is a certain subtle charm.

Approach to the Albigna valley will normally be made either from Vicosoprano or, more frequently, from Pranzaira where there is a cable-car used by maintenance staff working at the dam. This is also taken by climbers and walkers wishing to avoid the woodland walk from Vicosoprano. There is also a woodland path leading from Pranzaira that joins the Vicosoprano trail. This would have been very different in the days before the dam was built, for it led to the *Cascata*

Albigna Hut

dell' *Albigna*, which was '... a fine fall in a wild ravine'. The ravine is now dominated by the massive concrete wall towering overhead.

Route:20 Pranzaira (1,195m) - Albigna Hut (2,336m)

Grade: 2
Distance: 7 kilometres
Height gain: 1,141 metres
Time: 3½-4 hours

The Pranzaira cable-car takes about fifteen minutes to whisk passengers from the valley to the dam. The same distance occupies about three hours of walking time. But in the woods there's life and fragrance and always something of interest to study. It's a steep walk and the close-growing trees restrict the views, but such an approach to a wild region brings out the full impact of the mountain contrast.

Pranzaira will be found about two kilometres up-valley from Vicosoprano. Beside the road there is sufficient car parking space for a number of vehicles; also a Postbus stop. Walk uphill along the road for about 300 metres beyond the cable-car station until you come to a broad track turning off to the right. Follow this through the woods to reach the river, which here comes rushing through its great bed of granite blocks, and cross by way of a wooden footbridge. The track continues among lofty conifers, winding in large sweeps through the forest, then narrows to path-size. Shortly after this, another path (from Vicosoprano) comes from the right, and some time later a red and white paint flash indicates the point at which you leave the main path to join another climbing steeply to the right. This now leads in a consistently steep and lengthy haul up the rib that forms the western wall of the Albigna ravine.

On reaching the foot of the dam, cross below it to the eastern side by a continuing path, climb to the head of the wall (about 3 hours from Pranzaira) and find the hut path leading from the water's edge on the left. It climbs up the rough boulder slopes heading right, and reaches the Capanna da l'Albigna in about 35 minutes from the dam.

The Albigna hut commands a wild panorama; grey rocks and glaciers, snagged peaks all around, and the lake below. A popular place on account of its ease of access by cable-car from the valley, it sleeps 90 people - with room for 16 in the winter quarters - when the guardian is in residence. This is normally from mid-June until mid-September. Meals and drinks are then available.

Route 21: Vicosoprano (1,067m) - Albigna Hut (2,336m)

Grade: 2
Distance: 8 kilometres
Height gain: 1,269 metres
Time: 3½ hours

This route is an alternative to Route 20, and is recommended for its more leisurely initial approach, leading steadily up-valley through forest before beginning the stiff climb to the dam shared with Route 20 above. The path begins near Vicosoprano campsite, and follows along the true left bank of the Albigna river until it deserts it in favour of a climb in the shade of pines, eventually joining the path of the Pranzaira approach which comes from the left. Now follow Route 20 directions to the hut.

Route 22: Albigna Hut (2,336m) - Casnil Pass (2,975m) - Forno Hut (2,574m)

Grade: 3 (Some glacier crossing involved.)
Distance: 5.5 kilometres
Height gain: 639 metres   Height loss: 575 metres
Time: 4 hours

This crossing of the ridge wall that divides the Albigna and Forno valleys is not an unduly difficult one for experienced mountain trekkers. There are, in fact, two Casnil passes, but this route describes the passage of the northern one which is generally more used in summer. It has long been accepted as the standard link between the two valleys, and follows a rough track for most of the way.

Leave the Capanna da l'Albigna heading east on a clearly defined and well-trodden path, soon to break away on a left fork going northeast over a rough area of grass and rocks to reach a couple of little tarns in a small plateau under Piz dal Päl (2,618m). Cairns lead upward, now going east on a broad ridge, near the top of which bear left on a snowfield below the nameless peak shown as point 3,039m on the map. The pass is reached shortly after, with Piz Casnil rising above to the north. (This peak is reached by a one-hour scramble from the pass - grade II.) The view from the pass is very fine. (About 2-2½ hours from the hut.)

The descent into the Forno Valley is by way of a cairned track over snow and steep slopes of broken rocks, and it brings you to the edge of the Forno Glacier almost directly opposite the hut. Cross the glacier with care and join the main route to Capanna del Forno used by those ascending from Maloja.

Forno hut details are given under Route 4 description.

Saxifraga Oppositifolia

Piz de la Margna overlooking the lake of Silvaplana

Upper Engadine

UPPER ENGADINE
LAKES REGION

Suvretta da San

Piz Julier ▲

▲ Piz

JULIER PASS

SILVAPLA

Piz Lagrev ▲

SILS BASELGIA

GREVASALVAS ○

Lej dal Lunghin

SILS MAR

UPPER

Lej da Segl

○ ISOLA

Piz Lunghin ▲

MALOJA ○

Val Fedoz

Val Fex

Piz de la Margna ▲

Piz Muretto ▲

Fedoz Glacier

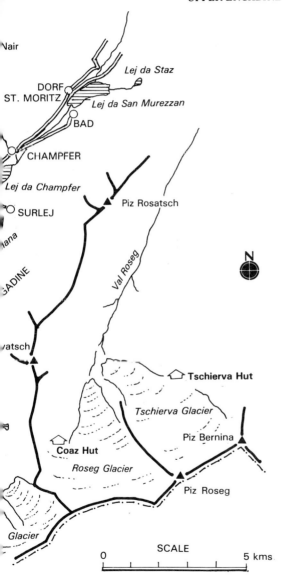

Nair

Lej da Staz

DORF
ST. MORITZ

Lej da San Murezzan

BAD

CHAMPFER

Lej da Champfer

SURLEJ

ana

GADINE

Val Roseg

N

Piz Rosatsch

atsch

Tschierva Hut

Tschierva Glacier

Coaz Hut

Piz Bernina

Roseg Glacier

Piz Roseg

Glacier

SCALE

0   5 kms.

63

From the head of the Maloja Pass at 1,805 metres, to the point where the valley becomes known as the Lower Engadine, is a distance of 39 kilometres and a drop in altitude of almost two hundred metres. In that distance the Upper Engadine *(Engiadina Ota,* or *Oberengadin)* changes in character from a broad, flat-bottomed lakeland to a more narrow, river-cut region of pasture and forest.

In its upper reaches, from Maloja to St. Moritz, four extensive lakes spread across the valley; the lakes of Sils, Silvaplana, Champfer and St. Moritz. In their waters dance reflections of the surrounding peaks. Forest of pine and larch come down to their shores on the right bank, while one community after another gazes out across the gleaming levels from the left bank. Over them all stands Piz de la Margna (3,158m), not a particularly high mountain, but one whose position and easily recognisable shape assures its pre-eminence.

The Val Bernina sweeps in from the south-east below St. Moritz, its milky glacial stream adding considerable strength to that of the Inn on the edge of the flood plain between Celerina and Samedan. The mountains here sacrifice their individuality for a series of ridges rucked with minor valleys and forests at their ankles. Only Piz Ketsch (3,417m) above Madulain is of interest to climbers, and that hides modestly from much of the Engadine's view.

A new road by-passes several of the more attractive villages here, and the tourist must forsake speed for the pleasures of cobbled streets in Zuoz, where ancient stone-walled houses crowd together in typical Engadine style, while above the village broad hillsides form a green backcloth. From Zuoz the old road leads through pastures above the river to S-chanf, then loses height gently with forest encroaching on either side until a sudden shaft on the left catches the eye, and there stretches the lovely Val Susauna, its charms well-disguised until you dare to tread deeper through its rather bland entrance. Beyond Val Susauna stands Cinuos-chel and the Lower Engadine. Another region with a character all its own.

Main Valley Bases:

Maloja (1,815m) stands at the head of the valley, ideally situated for the exploration of a number of side valleys, hillsides and walks alongside the Lake of Sils. It also overlooks the Val Bregaglia down the hairpins of the Maloja Pass. A straggling village, it has all the usual services; shops, bank, tourist information office, Post Office etc. It has hotel and *pension* accommodation, a Youth Hostel in its main street, and a campsite on the shores of the lake. To reach this, take the rough track that branches off the valley road at the southern end of the lake, and follow this round until you come to the campsite sign.

Silvaplana (1,815m) overlooks the lake of the same name to the south, and that of Champfer to the north. Opposite rises Piz Corvatsch with its cable-car, while behind the village twists the Julier Pass road. A well-contained village made more acceptable by the provision of a bypass which frees its street of too much traffic, it has hotels, restaurants, a campsite with first class facilities, and the usual shops and Post Office. Frequent Postbus services through the village, not only trans-Engadine routes, but also those that cross the Julier Pass towards Chur.

St. Moritz (1,822m) is an expensive resort conveniently divided between *Dorf* (the main town) and *Bad* (the spa section at the southern end of the lake). Whilst it has its undoubted attractions, architecturally St. Moritz is a brazen hybrid lacking in grace. However, it is extremely popular with visitors in both winter and summer, and lacks nothing in entertainment, shopping, accommodation, museums, sports facilities and mountains for wandering. It has a helpful tourist information centre with sufficient leaflets to keep you busy on a wet day. There are funiculars and cable-cars that could conveniently be used to gain height quickly up the mountainsides, there to begin your walk. And being at the railhead of the Rhaetian railway, there are trains frequently running down-valley to the Lower Engadine, or across to the Val Bernina and Poschiavo, or out of the region to Chur. Postbuses run daily almost everywhere. Both the Segantini and the Engadine Museum are worth visiting. There is a heated indoor swimming pool in St. Moritz Bad. In fact, plenty to occupy holiday makers when the weather keeps them off the hills. Although accommodation in hotels is likely to be very expensive, there is a Youth Hostel and also a campsite, both in St. Moritz Bad.

Pontresina (1,805m) is situated a short distance inside the Val Bernina and is linked with St. Moritz by train, Postbus and footpath. It looks directly into the superb Val Roseg, and is conveniently placed for excursions into the Morteratsch Valley, onto Piz Languard, the Val Muragl and various other good walking areas. Popular with climbers, Pontresina is also an ideal valley base from which to plan ascents among the nearby Bernina mountains. There is a guides' bureau and climbing school here. The shops and restaurants vie with those of St. Moritz, if marginally less expensive than their neighbour. There are many hotels; mostly expensive. But there's also a Youth Hostel near the railway station, camping at Punt Muragl and also up-valley near the entrance to the Morteratsch Valley. There is a tourist information office and all the usual services.

Samedan (1,720m) is the administrative 'capital' of the Engadine. It looks across the Inn-Bernina flood plain to the snow peaks of Piz Palü and the Bernina group in the south-east. A small but sturdy town, it has plenty of shops, Post Office, tourist information office, restaurants and a wide selection of hotels and *pension* accommodation. With rail connections for both the Engadine and Bernina lines, and the usual frequent Postbus services, Samedan is well situated for outings in many different regions covered by this guide. Across the valley from the town is the Engadine's small airport with its casual use by light aircraft and gliders. The Engadine's hospital is situated within the town.

Zuoz (1,716m) claims, with some justification, to be the best preserved village in the Upper Engadine with the characteristic vernacular architecture of its houses forming a splendid square. Certainly a much quieter place than those tourist towns and villages farther up-valley, it has a good selection of hotels and apartment houses for holiday rental, and all the usual shops and attractions such as open-air swimming pool. Conveniently situated for many walks, and with the National Park a short journey away, Zuoz has much to commend it as a valley base for a walking holiday.

Other Valley Bases:
Whilst those centres listed above are the main valley bases for the Upper Engadine, it would be true to say that practically every village has something to offer the discerning holiday maker, and there are hotels and/or *pensions* or apartments to rent in every community. *Sils Maria*, in the mouth of Val Fex, is attractive in its own right and superbly set among fine walking country. A little farther up-valley, and in its secluded lakeside position, *Isola* has limited *pension* accommodation in idyllic surroundings.

Champfer, between Silvaplana and St. Moritz, tends to be rather expensive, but has a superb view to Piz de la Margna and the lake-filled valley spread below. Its more recent buildings have followed traditional architectural styles in the main, and are a credit to their designers. *Sgraffito* ornamentation round the windows and doorways has reached a pinnacle of this particular art form here.

Down-valley from St. Moritz, *Celerina (Schlarigna)* is expanding fast. Plenty of accommodation here, but its immediate walks tend to be spoilt rather by the mechanical traceries of the winter ski industry marching over the hillsides.

Below Samedan, *Bever* lies at the junction of the Albula railway line. More modestly priced accommodation, and some good walking country nearby. Then, continuing down-valley, *La Punt - Chamues-ch* has the road, railway and river dividing this split community, quiet and often dismissed by the Engadine tourist; but *Madulain* has several interesting corners and some hotel accommodation. Immediately above this village footpaths lead to Piz Kesch. Other paths lead down to Zuoz through the sloping pastures, and beyond to *S-chanf,* the last village of any size in the Upper Engadine. There is a campsite nearby, opposite the entrance to Val Susauna, and in Val Susauna itself, a primitive Youth Hostel offering spartan accommodation, but with a delightful atmosphere.

Mountain Huts:
There are a number of huts scattered along the Upper Engadine, several of which are quite naturally situated in the Bernina massif. Some belong to the SAC, but others are privately owned, or in the hands of specific clubs. Beginning in the south and working down-valley, they are as follows: *Coaz Hut* (2,610m) high in the Val Roseg on the left bank of the Roseg Glacier, and across the valley but perched on the moraine wall of the Tschierva Glacier, is the *Tschierva Hut* (2,573m), a popular base for climbers tackling various routes on Piz Bernina, Piz Roseg and neighbouring peaks. To the east of the Tschierva Hut, and separated from it by the high ridge projecting northwards from Piz Bernina, lies the *Boval Hut* (2,495m) beside the Morteratsch Glacier. Nearby, with its superb panorama of the snow peaks running from Piz Palü to Bernina, is the privately owned *Diavolezza* (2,973m). Served by cable-car from the Val Bernina, this is an extremely busy restaurant by day in both summer and winter, but at night there is *matratzenlager* accommodation for climbers setting out for the big peaks rising beyond the glaciers to the south.

Above Pontresina, the *Georgyhutte* (3,176m) is a privately owned refuge just below the summit of Piz Languard, with a magnificent view across to the Bernina mountains. At the head of Val Bever, the *Jürg Jenatsch Hut* (2,652m), belonging to the Bernina Section of the SAC, is conveniently placed for climbs on lesser peaks, and for some strenuous walking tours. About 2½ hours of walking above Madulain brings you to the *Es-cha Hut* (2,594m) which serves Piz Kesch, while to the north of the mountain sits the *Kesch Hut* (2,632m), reached by a long approach from the Engadine that involves the crossing of one or two high passes.

UPPER ENGADINE ROUTES

The little hamlet of Isola

UPPER ENGADINE - LAKES REGION

Position:	From the head of the Maloja Pass to the junction of Val Bernina.
Maps:	Landeskarte der Schweiz 1:50,000 series No.268 'Julier Pass' 1:100,000 series No.44 'Maloja Pass' Kümmerly and Frey 'Wanderkarte-Oberengadin' 1:50,000
Valley Bases:	Maloja (1,815m), Sils Maria (1,800m), Silvaplana (1,815m), Champfer (1,825m), St. Moritz (1,822m)

A dazzling region of lakes, forest and high mountain, this section of the Engadine has so much to commend it as a centre for walking holidays. There are walks here to suit everyone's taste and ability amid some very fine mountain scenery. A region extremely rich in its alpine flora, the flower meadows through which a number of these paths lead will brighten any walker's day. There are glaciers and snowfields at the head of Val Fex; clear streams running everywhere, and little tarns on the hillsides as well as the extensive lakes of the main valley bed.

Alp hamlets like Grevasalvas and Blaunca sit on their hillside terraces seemingly lost to the world, and the tiny lakeside community of Isola below Val Fedoz is, as its name suggests, isolated from the remainder of the valley. Each of these is worth visiting on one or more of the walks outlined below.

In addition to valley walks described in this section, there are also routes given that lead high into the mountains, and one or two ascents of modest peaks suggested for the more adventurous and experienced of mountain walkers. All should be within the capabilities of fit and active ramblers with a reasonable amount of experience of mountain walking and scrambling.

Route 23: Maloja (1,815m) - Isola (1,812m) - Sils Maria (1,800m)

Grade:	1
Distance:	6.5 kilometres
Time:	1 hour 40 minutes

If you fancy an undemanding stroll in utterly delightful surroundings, then this is it. It is ideally suited to families with small children - even to the extent of being possible with a pushchair! - the path follows along the southern shore of the Lake of Sils (Silsersee), with larches

71

The path to Isola

overhanging in places, with shrubs and flowers everywhere, and lovely views along the lake with reflections of mountains dancing in it, or across to the shapely Piz Lagrev opposite. In early summer there's a constant fragrance from the shrubs newly freed from winter's burden of snow. In full summer it's no less delightful, but as with much of the walking in this valley, when the larches are turning gold towards the end of September, it is unforgettable.

Isola is a little hamlet secluded from the rest of the valley. It occupies a projection of pasture below the mouth of Val Fedoz, in the shadow of Piz de la Margna. A quiet community, extremely attractive in its simplicity, with a gushing waterfall bursting through the narrow gorge that almost closes Val Fedoz, and with views along the lake in both directions. The walk from Maloja passes through the hamlet and continues to Sils Maria, still beside the lake, and from Sils one can take a Postbus back to Maloja.

A broad track leaves Maloja alongside the Schweizerhaus and goes to the lakeside. Another comes from the main Engadine road at the southern end of the lake, for those who might be coming from other parts of the valley. Car parking is possible a short distance along this track.

Follow the lakeside track round towards the wooded slopes of the valley, continuing towards Isola seen ahead. The track divides after a short stretch. A more narrow path leaves to the left and wanders along the very water's edge, rising and falling here and there, and is well worth taking for the intimacy of the views and the lush shrubbery it passes through. It joins the main track again before entering Isola. In Isola there are refreshments available at a *pension*/restaurant. Continue in the same direction along the water's edge to reach Sils Maria.

Route 24:   Maloja (1,815m) - Piz de la Margna (3,158m)

Grade: 3
Distance: 5 kilometres
Height gain: 1,343 metres
Time: 4 hours

The ascent of Piz de la Margna is included in this walking guide as it involves little technical climbing ability, and should be within the scope of most *experienced* mountain walkers. The views from the summit are quite magnificent, looking as they do not only along the Engadine in a huge sweep of lake and valley and pasture, but also over the Bernina snow peaks and to that graceful mountain, Monte Disgrazia, standing aloof and elegant across the Muretto Pass; then south to the Bregaglia peaks and glaciers.

A note to consider here, before the route is given; an ice axe will be necessary early in the summer when there is still much snow and ice lying towards the summit. But later, in a normal year, the ascent should be quite feasible without any additional equipment. Since the mountain is clearly seen from so many positions in the Upper Engadine, it should be possible to ascertain the degree of snow cover long before a decision is made whether to set out to climb it.

Take Route 23 along the lakeside until an obvious broad track forks off to the right and climbs the flank of mountain towards Val Fedoz. This is the track to take. It leads into Val Fedoz and makes for the huts of Cadsternam, but just before reaching these, it is joined by another path coming from the left (from Sils Maria). A path breaks away to the south (right) immediately after the huts, and climbs rough grass slopes, quite steeply to reach screes and slips of snow. A little stream is seen, and just before reaching this you leave the path and head up over grass and screes to the right in a steeply sloping little valley. There is a vague path to follow. This leads onto a broad saddle in the north-east ridge of the mountain. Now go up the rocky ridge without difficulty, directly to the summit.

Allow 2-2½ hours for the descent.

Route 25: Maloja (1,815m) - Piz Lunghin (2,780m)

Grade: 3
Distance: 3 kilometres
Height gain: 965 metres
Time: 3-3½ hours

Another easy mountain, Piz Lunghin stands to the west of Maloja and is so prominently situated as to give remarkable panoramas over the Bregaglia and Engadine. No technical difficulties should be encountered under normal summer conditions.

Follow Route 5 from Maloja to the saddle of the Lunghin Pass (2,645m); a walk of about two and a half hours or so. At the pass a path branches off to the left, and is signposted to 'Piz Lunghin'. It leads in a steep winding trail without difficulty up the craggy rocks directly to the summit, in about half an hour from the pass.

Allow about two hours for the descent.

Route 26: Plaun da Lej (1,805m) - Grevasalvas (1,941m) - Blaunca (2,037m) - Maloja (1,815m)

Grade: 1
Distance: 6 kilometres
Height gain: 232 metres   Height loss: 222 metres
Time: 1½ hours

This walk leads up to a hidden shelf of mountainside above the Engadine's left bank, and explores two tiny alp hamlets that time seems to have passed by. Now and again there are surprise views across the valley to Piz Corvatsch with the Lake of Sils deep below. A good path is followed all the way from Plaun da Lej, which is in itself an attractive lakeside area halfway along the Lake of Sils, and served by Postbus from either Maloja or villages to the north along the valley. Refreshments are available here at a restaurant that revels in its glorious views.

Take the motorable track (only authorised vehicles may use this) which leads behind the restaurant at Plaun da Lej and winds up the hillside. At a fork turn right and continue until you come to the hamlet of Grevasalvas nestling among undulating pastures, its old grey stone buildings appearing to be as much a part of the landscape as the mountains rising out of it. From Grevasalvas bear left and take the path that does a sweep of a bend, then straightens out to reach an even smaller hamlet, that of Blaunca. The path goes between the houses and continues over an almost moorland stretch of hillside, with views off to the left over the Engadine. It eventually leads down to the village of Maloja.

Route 27: Julier Pass (2,284m) - Fuorcla Grevasalvas (2,688m) - Plaun da Lej (1,805m)

Grade: 2
Distance: 8 kilometres
Height gain: 455 metres   Height loss: 883 metres
Time: 3-3½ hours

An interesting outing, this is, it gives a considerable variety of scenery, the highlight of which is the sudden vista on emerging from the Fuorcla Grevasalvas with the distant snows of Bernina rising in dramatic form beyond the intervening ridges of Corvatsch, with the depths of the Engadine dazzling their lakes far below. Take the Postbus to the Julier Hospice in the morning, and wander at leisure back to the Engadine.

From the point marked La Vaduta on the map, found on the far side of the Julier Pass, a path branches away from the road to the south (left) and wanders up the grassy hillside - a somewhat bleak place - to reach a small tarn known as Lej Grevasalvas (2,390m) below the northern crags of Piz Lagrev. Pass to the right of the tarn and follow the stream leading through the valley, going straight ahead up to the pass slung between Piz d'Emmat-Dadaint and Piz Lagrev. On emerging through this saddle, the route now drops steeply over rough ground, eventually to reach the hamlet of Grevasalvas, then down the winding track to Plaun da Lej and the Engadine road.

Route 28: Sils Baselgia (1,799m) - Grevasalvas (1,941m) - Maloja (1,815m)

Grade: 2
Distance: 7.5 kilometres
Height gain: 240 metres   Height loss: 224 metres
Time: 2 hours

There is a fine footpath which runs along the northern side of the valley from St. Moritz to Maloja, known as the *Via Engiadina*. The full route is detailed below (Route 40), but this walk is a portion of that longer route and is recommended as an evening stroll, or to fill an afternoon. It may also be used conveniently as an extension of Route 23, thereby creating a circular outing of considerable charm. As a walk on its own, the Postbus service makes it possible to either reach the start of the walk, or return from its completion.

The path begins beside the main Engadine road opposite the turning for Sils Baselgia at the north-eastern end of the Lake of Sils. Head left as the path begins to gain height steadily into trees on the long traverse south-westward. It is a clear path offering no difficulties; even where it crosses a boulder slope, typical Swiss efficiency has created a gentle continuing path, level and even under foot. Above Grevasalvas it narrows a little to cross a minor 'pass' in a spur of the mountain, and on the westward side of it you gain a splendid view of the hamlet lying below. The path drops down, crosses the pastures into Grevasalvas, and continues along the trail to Blaunca, over the semi-moorland hillside and down again through Pila to Maloja.

Route 29: Sils Maria (1,800m) - Val Fex - Plaun Vadret (2,122m)

Grade: 1
Distance: 8 kilometres
Height gain: 322 metres
Time: 3-3½ hours

Val Fex is one of the loveliest of the side valleys feeding into the Upper Engadine. It's a green and gentle vale with soft pastures leading to scenes of glaciers and snowfields at its head. Just inside the valley the houses of Fex Crasta are dotted across the meadows, and the little white church, so neat and cared-for, makes a delightful picture with the mountains rising behind it. In the graveyard lies Christian Klucker (1853-1928), one of the finest mountain guides of his day, who lived most of his life in the valley, and it was at the age of only six that he first went to work for his father as a cowherd '...amongst the beautiful flowering pastures of the Fextal'. Nowadays walkers in this tranquil valley may well see the young successors of Christian Klucker watching over their cattle through the long days of summer.

It might be of interest to note here that many of the cows seen grazing in the Engadine and adjacent valleys, do not belong to local farmers, but are sent from the lowlands of Switzerland by train early in the summer, and are tended by Engadine cowherds for the best weeks of the year. Feeding on the rich Engadine grasses is extremely beneficial to them, and whilst they are here, lowland farmers can put their land to use in growing crops whilst their cattle are enjoying a long holiday in the mountains and being fattened for the coming winter. The arrival of the cattle trains in the summer is a spectacle worth rising early for, as large herds of cows are led through the streets of St. Moritz and neighbouring villages on their way to pasture. Val Fex is one of the valleys where migrant cattle come to graze, and the pastures will be ringing with their bells.

This walk is a gentle one. It follows for much of the way a broad motorable track. This, however, is for locals and permit holders only; the sole tourist 'traffic' allowed being horse-drawn open carriages hired from Sils Maria. This is where the walk begins, in the car park in the square where the village street makes an abrupt bend.

Take the footpath signposted 'Val Fex' as it heads into a narrow gorge and gains height along a covered section of path, protected by a wooden handrail. It brings you out among farm houses and haybarns at Platta, crosses the river and shortly after joins the broad track. Bear left and follow this along the valley, enjoying the views that entice you on, past the little church, then through the pastures to a small hamlet called Curtins. Not far beyond Curtins the track reaches a hotel, and from this point the track makes way for a more narrow path. Continue along the valley with the river still on your right, then cross the bridge to the other side.

The path now takes you deeper into the valley, and a little under two kilometres after having crossed the river, you reach a little tarn with an alp hut beside it. Plaun Vadret lies immediately beyond, with streams running through from the glaciers directly ahead, (Plaun Vadret means simply the plain of the glaciers) and from those hanging above to the left, spilling over from the huge icefield formed beyond the Fuorcla Fex-Scerscen across which runs the Italian border.

Route 30: Sils Maria (1,800m) - Curtins (1,973m) - Marmorè (2,199m) - Sils Maria

Grade: 2
Distance: 8 kilometres
Height gain: 399 metres   Height loss: 399 metres
Time: 3-3½ hours

This walk makes a very pleasant circuit beginning and ending in Sils. It explores the Val Fex as far as the hamlet of Curtins, enjoying as it does the pastoral nature of the valley which contrasts markedly with the world of snow and ice hanging at the end of the valley. Then from Curtins the route returns on itself, wandering the hillside to the north and heading back on a steadily climbing path to the viewpoint of Marmorè which overlooks the toy-like houses of Fex Crasta below, and peers into the upper reaches of the Engadine. This is a flowery stretch of hillside, especially rich in primulas and dwarf azaleas that form a lush carpet. The descent from Marmorè to Sils Maria is a steep one, but it's not difficult, although if you have young children with you, or you are inadequately shod, take care on the descending path.

Follow Route 29 from the car park at Sils Maria through Val Fex to Curtins. Now take the path which branches away from the main track to the left. It climbs up the hillside with a stream on your right, then heads left on a rising traverse towards a rocky 'gateway' ahead. The path is clearly marked all the way, and at Marmorè, which is no more than a belvedere on top of a cliff where alternative paths lead away, go straight ahead ignoring the path which heads off to the right. Descend through a lush vegetation, and later among trees, in a series of zig-zags that eventually return you to Sils Maria once more.

Route 31: Sils Maria (1,800m) - Marmorè (2,199m) - Lej Sgrischus (2,618m) - Piz Chüern (2,689m) - Curtins (1,973m) - Sils Maria

Grade: 2
Distance: 13 kilometres
Height gain: 889 metres   Height loss: 889 metres
Time: 6 hours

This rather strenuous, yet rewarding circuit, takes in a number of fine viewpoints, and has been a popular outing among the more adventurous of walkers for many years. Nowadays it is possible to take the cable-car from Sils to Prasüra (2,313m) (the Furtschellas cableway) and join this route above Marmorè, thereby saving about an hour's stiff walking. Whichever way you choose to do the circuit, wait for a fine spell of settled weather, and take your camera along.

The path starts by the Hotel Edelweiss in Sils Maria, and climbs steeply through forest and shrubbery, emerging to open hillside shortly before reaching the clifftop viewpoint of Marmorè, in about an hour. Take the path ahead as it climbs the crest of Alp Munt, working south-eastwards across hillsides to the little hut of Munt Sura (2,439m). Shortly after having passed this, the path zig-zags half-left and reaches the bowl in which nests the tarn, Lej Sgrischus. (About 2½ hours from Sils.) Having reached the tarn's northern shore, our path quickly deserts it to climb a further seventy metres up to the summit of Piz Chüern, with its fine lookout over the Val Fex to Piz de la Margna and the snowy head of the valley to the south.

From Piz Chüern the route now drops to the south, then bears right to work its way steadily down to the terrace of hillside above Curtins, before joining the main hillside traverse that leads to the hamlet in the bed of Val Fex. The broad valley track now leads through Fex and back to Sils Maria once more. A splendid day's outing.

Route 32: Sils Maria (1,800m) - Prasüra (2,318m) - Lej de la Fuorcla (2,489m) - Hahnensee (2,153m) - St. Moritz Bad (1,772m)

Grade: 2
Distance: 13 kilometres
Height gain: 689 metres   Height loss: 717 metres
Time: 4½-5 hours

This is a high-level walk on hillsides that give views along the Engadine, and steeply down into the lakes below. It's a walk that has plenty of variety, and one that could be shortened by taking the Furtschellas cable-car from Sils, thereby saving about an hour's walking. Refreshments are available at Hahnensee (shown as Lej dals Chöds on the map).

Take the path towards Marmorè from Hotel Edelweiss in Sils Maria, (beginning of Route 31) and upon arrival at this splendid cliff-top belvedere, take the path to Prasüra where the cableway terminates. The path climbs above it, then bears left to follow round the hillside on a path which heads for Fuorcla Surlej; the pass which gives access to Val Roseg. Continue along this path, ignoring alternatives to right and left. The path eventually leads into a rather desolate hanging valley below Fuorcla Surlej, with the middle station (Murtel) of the Corvatsch cableway above to the right.

Cross the valley, passing beside the little tarn of Lej da la Fuorcla, and then take the left-hand path seen cutting across the hillside ahead. This brings you to a more lush vegetated hillside, with shrubs and trees and direct views off to the sprawl of St. Moritz in the valley ahead. Shortly before reaching Hahnensee, look back along the valley towards Sils, where there is a wonderful view of lakes and mountains framed by the rich shrubbery. On reaching the secluded tarn of Hahnensee, with its restaurant offering welcome refreshment, there is a choice of routes. One leads left to Surlej and Silvaplana; one drops down to Champfèr, while another heads north-eastwards through the trees to St. Moritz. This brings you to one of several points in St. Moritz Bad where Postbuses will return you along the valley to Sils.

Route 33:   Sils Maria (1,800m) - Fuorcla Surlej (2,755m) -
Val Roseg - Pontresina (1,805m)

Grade: 2
Distance: 18 kilometres
Height gain: 955 metres   Heigt loss: 950 metres
Time: 6½ hours

One of the classic views of the Upper Engadine is that which looks out from the vantage point of Fuorcla Surlej across the depths of Val Roseg to the magnificent ice-coated savage peaks of Piz Bernina and Piz Roseg, their great hanging glaciers perched precariously above the turmoil of icefields and bowls of snow. It is a view that adorns many a Swiss calendar, but no amount of familiarity can detract from the grandeur of the scene, and it is this which makes a highlight of the walk.

The walk itself is a long and tiring one. Again, as with several others described, it may be shortened by taking the cable-car to Furtschellas, or even that which goes from Surlej near Silvaplana to Corvatsch (alight at the middle station). But those who complete the walk from Sils to Pontresina will certainly feel that it has been worth the effort.

Take Route 32 to the pathway leading from Prasüra to Lej da la Fuorcla. On reaching the spur of mountain that houses the Corvatsch cableway middle station, turn right and climb up to it, then continue beyond on a clear broad path that takes you directly to the saddle of Fuorcla Surlej. (About 3¾ hours from Sils.) There is a restaurant here where refreshments may be bought and consumed with that wonderful panorama spread before you. *(Matratzenlager* accommodation also available, but more expensive than at SAC huts.)

Dropping down on the eastern side the path divides. That which heads right goes to the Coaz hut. The left-hand trail leads down to Hotel Roseg by way of a couple of alps. This is the path to take. It is a splendid path for it has Piz Bernina and Piz Roseg beaming across the valley. It has flowers and grazing cattle and fresh scent of the valley drifting in the breeze. An easily graded path, on reaching the valley floor there is once more the opportunity for refreshment at Hotel Roseg.

From the hotel the main track heads down-valley to Pontresina. After a short spell the way divides. The main track goes left, soon to

Bernina and Piz Roseg from Fuorcla Surlej

cross the river to its left bank, while a more narrow path stays with the right bank. Both lead to Pontresina and emerge near the railway station.

Return to Sils by train to St. Moritz, then Postbus up-valley.

Route 34: Sils Maria (1,800m) - Chastè - Sils Baselgia (1,799m)

Grade: 1
Distance: 3.5 kilometres
Time: 1½ hours

Sils Maria and Sils Baselgia are separated by a marshy plain drained by two rivers. To the west lies the lovely Lake of Sils, and projecting into it, roughly halfway between Maria and Baselgia, is a narrow wooded promontory called Chastè. A footpath leads around this, affording as it does some delightful views over the lake to the walling mountains. This path is a very popular one, for it can be enjoyed by young and old alike. There's practically no height gain to tax the lungs or legs, but there are flowering plants and shrubs beside the path, and red squirrels scampering along the branches of pine trees overhead, and the gentle lap-lap of the water splashing against the shoreline, and the shapely Piz de la Margna dancing a reflection before you. If you wake early one summer morning, rise quietly and enjoy this walk before breakfast. Alternatively, wander it on a soft evening after dinner when shadows are falling and swifts dart low over the water. You'll share the stillness with fishermen quietly gazing at their lines from a mid-lake rowing boat.

Take the path from Sils Maria either directly across the plain to Chastè, or first down to the lakeside and follow the water's edge north-westward along the end of the lake until you reach a junction of paths at the wooded promontory. Turn left and keep with the path as it makes its circuit of the projection, finally leading off to Sils Baselgia or, if preferred, back to Maria.

Route 35: Sils Maria (1,800m) - Surlej (1,809m) - Silvaplana (1,815m)

Grade: 1
Distance: 6 kilometres
Time: 2 hours

Another easy lakeside walk, this follows along the right bank of the Lake of Silvaplana, enjoying the views, the fragrance of shrubs and pine trees and the gentle lapping of the water.

From Sils Maria walk to the valley station of the Furtschellas cableway, and take the path which leads from it to the lakeside. The path continues without difficulty or diversion all the way to the bridge leading from Surlej to Silvaplana by the strange castle-like building of Crap da Sass. Cross the bridge and walk alongside the road into Silvaplana village where Postbuses are found outside the Post Office in the main street. (Turn right on reaching the village street. The Post Office is a few metres along this.)

Route 36: Silvaplana (1,815m) - Lej da la Tscheppa (2,626m) - Silvaplana

Grade: 2
Distance: 9 kilometres
Height gain: 811 metres   Height loss: 811 metres
Time: 5 hours

Lej da la Tscheppa occupies a rocky bowl high above the valley, and this walk is a strenuous circuit that leads to it, enjoying along the way some quite delightful views over the valley to Piz de la Margna and Piz Corvatsch. It's marmot country, so keep an eye alert for these furry creatures bounding among the rocks.

Leave Silvaplana by way of a path which cuts left from the main Julier Pass road as it makes a sharp elbow turn to the right on the edge of the village. The path immediately crosses the river (Ova dal Vallun) draining from the Julier, and works its way up the hillside until it is joined by another from the right. Now head left to climb numerous tight zig-zags up to a stony mountainside, following the path all the way. It reaches the lake after about 3½ hours, just comes to the south-eastern shore, and leaves immediately by heading left alongside the stream which flows from it. Shortly before dropping to the road the path divides. Right leads along the *Via Engiadina* (Route 40) to Sils and Maloja, left to Silvaplana, straight on to reach the Lake of Silva-plana. Bear left and follow the traversing path back to the village.

Route 37: Silvaplana (1,815m) - Fuorcla Surlej (2,755m) - Val Roseg - Pontresina (1,805m)

Grade: 2
Distance: 18 kilometres
Height gain: 940 metres   Height loss: 950 metres
Time: 6½ hours

This is a variation of Route 33, one of the classic Upper Engadine outings. Although it doesn't have the benefit of the hillside walk that begins the Sils Maria - Fuorcla Surlej crossing, it does have a pleasant initial climb through the woods above Surlej to Alp Surlej (2,096m). Yet again, this is another route that can be shortened by as much as three hours by taking the Corvatsch cable-car to its middle station.

Cross the valley by road from Silvaplana to Surlej, and take the second path to the right, about halfway through the development of Surlej, and follow this through the trees, steadily gaining height until you reach the buildings of Alp Surlej about an hour after setting off from Silvaplana. Above the alp the path winds steeply, passes another alp (Margun) and on to the cable-car station. From here follow directions as for Route 33.

Route 38: Silvaplana (1,815m) - Pass Suvretta (2,615m) - Piz Nair (3,057m)

Grade: 2
Distance: 10 kilometres
Height gain: 1,242 metres
Time: 4½ hours

In winter Piz Nair is a very popular ski mountain with the St. Moritz crowd. There is a cable-car to the summit, on which a large statue of an ibex peers down into the valley. This route for a summer walk leads up the valley of Suvretta da San Murezzan, down which skiers come hurtling for about five months of the year. Traffic is not quite so numerous or boisterous in summer.

Take the path which leaves Silvaplana main street on the edge of the Julier Pass road and head to the right (north) out of the village. On two or three occasions it passes close by the Julier road before gaining height in zig-zags and then traversing to the right round the hillside and into the valley of Suvretta da San Murezzan in one and a half hours. (San Murezzan, incidentally, is Romansch for St. Moritz.)

Continue through the valley on a clear path which follows the stream right to the little tarn (Lej Suvretta) tucked just below the pass. From the pass itself a path heads off to the right, then forks left to climb in long sweeps the fine cone of the mountain as far as the summit restaurant and cable-car station. Either return the same way (allowing 3 hours for the descent), or take the cable-car to Corviglia where a funicular runs down to St. Moritz, and Postbus to Silvaplana.

Route 39:   Silvaplana (1,815m) - Lej Marsch (1,818m) -
Lej Nair (1,864m) - Silvaplana

Grade: 1
Distance: 5 kilometres
Height gain: 49 metres
Time: 1½ hours

This is an early morning walk; the earlier the better. With the sun just up there's a stillness in the air, and as the walk first leads alongside the Lake of Champfer there may well be the flash of trout leaping from the water. Then into the woods where if you walk quietly, there's every possibility of catching sight of deer or chamois grazing in the clearings. Both tarns of Lej Marsch and Lej Nair are good places to observe animals coming down to drink in the cool quiet of early morning, and several times I have sat there among the shrubbery as both red and roe deer have grazed only a few metres from me.

Cross the bridge leading from Silvaplana to Surlej, and immediately after take the path heading left towards the woods. On reaching these follow the left-hand track alongside the lake, which is never seen in a better light than that of early morning. When the lake finishes, continue ahead beside the River Inn, but then fork right to Lej Marsch, a small tarn surrounded by forest trees. Ignore the first path to the right, but take the second which climbs among trees and brings you to the clearing in which sits Lej Nair. There is a path on either side of this. Take that which goes to the right, and follow it back to the Surlej-Silvaplana road.

Route 40:   St. Moritz (1,822m) - Alp Suvretta (2,211m) - Val Güglia - Grevasalvas (1,941m) - Maloja (1,815m)

Grade: 2
Distance: 19 kilometres
Height gain: 389 metres (or 29 metres with use of cable-car)
Time: 6-7 hours

The *Via Engiadina* is the Upper Engadine equivalent of the Bregaglia's *Sentiero panoramico* (Route 10). A lengthy traverse of the hillsides bordering the northern side of the valley, by linking a number of existing footpaths this walk was created and signposted as a positive encouragement to visitors. It is a moderately easy ramble on a well-graded path, and with opportunities to drop down to the valley at various points along the way should the weather change during the walk, or to make a shorter day of it.

The route begins at the top station of the Signal cableway which rises from St. Moritz Bad near the Post Office. There is a walker's ticket *(Wanderbillette)* available that combines the St. Moritz-Signal cableway, and return from Maloja on the Postbus, thereby making a financial saving. (A similar ticket is available for intermediate stages, returning from Silvaplana or Sils Baselgia.)

For those who would prefer to walk all the way, thus avoiding the Signal cable-car, start in the square at St. Moritz Dorf, walk up to Chantarella (or travel by funicular) and take the path heading across the hillside south-westwards to reach the green shoulder of Alp Giop where the Signal cable-car terminates.

The *Via Engiadina* footpath leads from the Signal station round to the south-west to enter the valley of Suvretta da San Murezzan seen ahead. The path crosses this by Alp Suvretta and continues to work its way below the contorted lump of Piz Albana, and to pass above Silvaplana. Cross the Julier Pass road and descend towards the valley before resuming the traverse towards Sils. With fine views up-valley to Piz de la Margna seen rising above the lakes, the trail reaches a junction with the path from Sils Baselgia after about four hours. It then carries on through sparse trees, crosses a boulder slope and rises gently to go through a minor pass before dropping down into the little alp hamlet of Grevasalvas. The path from here winds up to the few stone dwellings that comprise the hamlet of Blaunca, then over a semi-moorland hillside and drops down through Pila to the valley floor at Maloja.

Route 41: St. Moritz (1,822m) - Alp Suvretta (2,211m) - Pass Suvretta (2,615m) - Val Bever - Bever (1,708m)

Grade: 2
Distance: 21 kilometres
Height gain: 793 metres   Height loss: 907 metres
Time: 7-7½ hours

A long, but interesting walk, this is a circuit of the mountain mass formed by a ridge of minor peaks running from Piz Nair to Piz Ot above St. Mortiz and Samedan. It may be considerably shortened by use of the cable-car from St. Moritz Bad to Signal at Alp Giop (saving perhaps an hour), or by use of a combination of funicular (St. Moritz Dorf to Corviglia) and cable-car to Piz Nair (from Corviglia), thus saving about three hours of walking.

Follow directions as for Route 40 as far as Alp Suvretta, which will be reached in about two hours from St. Moritz Dorf. From here turn right and head straight up the valley to reach the summit of the pass in a further hour and a quarter. Piz Nair is above to the right, Piz Suvretta to the left, the lovely 'armchair' shape of the glaciated corries of Piz Julier behind. Cross over the pass and walk down the next Val Suvretta (both sides of the pass share this name), here being the valley of Suvretta da Samedan.

The path follows a stream down to a short distance before it flows into the Beverin stream at the junction with Val Bever. This junction is known, rather confusedly, as Alp Suvretta too, and is reached in about five hours or so from St. Moritz. (The Jürg Jenatsch Hut lies some distance up-valley to the left.) Bear right a little above the huts of Alp Suvretta on the path to Bever. It slopes down to meet and cross the stream, and wanders along the left bank all the way into the Engadine at Bever. (Train or Postbus back to St. Moritz.)

Route 42: St. Moritz (Corviglia) (2,486m) - Alp Laret (2,103m) - St. Moritz (1,822m)

Grade: 1
Distance: 3.5 kilometres
Height loss: 664 metres
Time: 1½ hours

A short walk, mostly downhill all the way from the Corviglia funicular station, this excursion gives surprising views off to the snow giants of Piz Palü and Bellavista out to the south. Since the walk up to Corviglia has little to commend it, the suggestion is offered to ride the funicular and begin the walk from its upper station.

A number of paths spread out from Corviglia, but the one to take is that which heads directly off to the right and goes behind the minor ridge heading north-east. After a short stroll another path cuts off from this to the right. Ignore this, but continue ahead, passing beyond the point of Sass da Muottas (2,364m), heading down the slope until you reach a crossing path where you must turn right. Follow this to Alp Laret and beyond it, passing the radio tower, and down then to reach St. Moritz Dorf.

**Route 43: St. Moritz (1,822m) - Surlej (1,809m) -
Sils Maria (1,800m) - Maloja (1,815m)**

Grade: 1
Distance: 21 kilometres
Time: 5½-6 hours

This walk links the major lakes of the Upper Engadine in a delightful day's outing. It is not a difficult one; there are no steep gradients to contend with, and at several points it is possible to terminate the walk and catch a Postbus back to St. Moritz. At any time of the year this is an attractive ramble. Even in winter it is fine, for one can dispense with normal footpaths and wander across the centre of the frozen lakes from one end of the valley to the other. In summer, of course, there are reflections for company; the occasional flash of leaping trout, fishermen quietly contemplating the waters, sailboard enthusiasts colouring the lakes, and the glorious fragrance of shoreline shrubbery and forest.

Cross the road below St. Moritz Dorf near the railway station and take the footpath which leads left along the edge of the lake, and takes you across to the southern side, where pine and larch woods come down almost to the water. The path leads along to St. Moritz Bad where you can either walk through the town on the road leading towards Maloja, or take the path round by the large spa hotels to the left, with forest immediately behind them. Either way, make for the campsite which will be found near the ski jump *(Olympiaschanze)*. On reaching the campsite take the path alongside the river, heading upstream. This will bring you to the lakeside of Lej da Champfer.

On reaching the end of Champfer lake, cross the grassy pasture in which a number of attractive houses have been built (this is Surlej), go over the road which joins Surlej and Silvaplana, and passing the curious orange-roofed castle-like building of Crap da Sass to your right, continue ahead on the path which runs along the southern shore of the Lake of Silvaplana. There are lovely views ahead.

From the southern end of this lake continue to Sils Maria by either of two paths. In Sils Maria itself follow the road as it makes a sharp elbow turn to the right towards Sils Baselgia across the valley, then break away to the left shortly after on a footpath which leads directly to the shoreline of the largest of the four lakes, that of Silsersee *(Lej da Segl)*. In many ways this is the best of all to walk beside. Halfway along it you come to the delta formed by the river gushing from Val Fedoz, bringing with it soil and rock debris from the mountains. Tucked on this green pasture is the hamlet of Isola; superbly set with its gentle views of peak, pasture and lake. Refreshments are available here. The continuing path will occupy about an hour's walking into Maloja.

Route 44:   St. Moritz (1,822m) - Piz da l'Ova-Cotschna (2,716m)

Grade: 2
Distance: 4 kilometres
Height gain: 894 metres
Time: 2¾ hours

Looking across the valley from St. Moritz the mountain which forms the south-eastern wall, and which catches the glow of evening, is Piz Rosatsch (3,123m). In effect, Rosatsch is made up of several peaklets forming individual features on a broad massif. This massif drops at its southern end to the saddle of Fuorcla Surlej. Whilst the Rosatsch massif certainly has little of interest to climbers, it does have a number of easily accessible points from which one receives entertaining views. From Piz Mezdi (2,992m), for example, there are fine panoramas of the Bernina group and of the Engadine shafting away to the north. Rosatsch itself has similar views, although a little more extensive than those of Mezdi. But the lesser point of Piz da l'Ova-Cotschna - hardly a peaklet, but a lump below the glacial corrie of Rosatsch - provides a short ascent with little features all its own, as well as a splendid belvedere from which to study the area immediately below. Go early in the day and stay alert for a sighting of chamois or marmots.

The path begins behind the French church near the *Heilbad* in St.

Moritz Bad. Several paths start from here, but that which we must take climbs ahead into the forest by tight zig-zags to reach the main traversing path. Bear left here and follow this a short distance before forking right. For much of the ascent it shares the same route as that for Piz Mezdi, but on reaching a rib that forms the eastern wall of a steep little valley, go up it until you see a small tarn on your right. This is Lej da l'Ova-Cotschna. Cross to the tarn, which is set in a rocky bowl, and go up to the viewpoint of Piz da l'Ova-Cotschna on the other side.

Route 45:   St. Moritz (1,822m) - Hahnensee (2,153m) -
Fuorcla Surlej (2,755m) - Val Roseg -
Pontresina (1,805m)

Grade: 2
Distance: 18 kilometres
Height gain: 933 metres   Height loss: 950 metres
Time: 5½-6 hours

Another variation of Route 33, the classic crossing of the saddle of Fuorcla Surlej, with its spectacular views, into Val Roseg. Once again, it is possible to foreshorten the walk by taking the Corvatsch cable-car from Surlej to the middle station, thereby saving a little more than two and a half hours. But the walk up from St. Moritz through the woods to the little tarn of Hahnensee (Lej dals Chöds) with its neat restaurant, makes a lovely stroll in its own right, and a good start to a long and ever-interesting day's exercise.

Take the path which begins by the French church near the *Heilbad* in St. Moritz Bad. It is signposted to Hahnensee and Fuorcla Surlej. Follow as it climbs steadily among trees up-valley, gaining height on the slopes of the Rosatsch massif, until you reach the restaurant and tarn of Hahnensee after about 1¼ hours. Just beyond Hahnensee there is a lovely view down to the Engadine lakes.

From the tarn the route now bears round to the south, rising soon over the open mountainside, and enters the barren hanging valley which leads up to Fuorcla Surlej. Across the valley stands the middle station of the Corvatsch cableway, and there you'll find all the sad evidence of winter skiing left here through the summer as a scar on the hillside. (If only it were possible to dismantle ski-tows when the season is over, so that the hillsides may regain some of their former glory!) The path climbs without difficulty to the saddle of Fuorcla Surlej, which is reached in about 3¼ hours from St. Moritz Bad. To continue, follow Route 33 to Pontresina.

Route 46:   St. Moritz (1,822) - Lej da Staz (1,809m) -
Pontresina (1,805m)

Grade: 1
Distance: 5.5 kilometres
Time: 1¼ hours

This is one of those pleasant, undemanding rambles that makes such good use of half a day. There are many like this throughout the Engadine. Wander across pastures and through sparse woods on an easy-graded path as far as Pontresina, there to explore this resort, or to extend the day with a walk in the Val Roseg, or perhaps take the chair lift above the town and enjoy the views. Both Postbus and train offer convenient return transport to St. Moritz if you do not feel like retracing your footsteps along this path homeward. On the way there is the possibility of catching sight of deer among the trees, or, in early morning or evening, grazing in the open.

Go down to the northern end of the lake below St. Moritz, and wander along the shoreline path towards the woods on the far side. On reaching these take the path left, which will lead to the little tarn of Stazersee *(Lej da Staz)*. Refreshments are available here at the restaurant overlooking the lake from the north-eastern end.

Now take the path immediately behind the restaurant, heading off to the right (east) into the woods. Follow this all the way to Pontresina railway station. The town is reached by way of the road. Val Roseg is the enchanting valley branching away behind the railway station, and is well worth exploring. (See Routes 48, 49 and 50.)

Route 47:   St. Moritz (1,822m) - Alp da Staz (1,942m) -
Lej da Staz (1,809m) - St. Moritz

Grade: 1
Distance: 8.5 kilometres
Height gain: 120 metres   Height loss: 120 metres
Time: 2¼ hours

Whilst Alp Staz lies only two kilometres away from the heart of St. Moritz, it is, in reality, a world away from the fashionable boutiques, the casino and restaurants and high-class hotels. Alp Staz belongs to that other Switzerland; the Switzerland of romantic simplicity, of pastoral nostalgia. The path which runs a little above the alp looks down on it and encompasses in one glance the full contrast of alp hut and grand hotel. It is a view that is full of anachronisms. The walk itself makes a fair afternoon's exercise, and there are always refreshments to be had at Stazersee *(Lej da Staz)*.

Cross the valley in St. Moritz Bad to the south side, passing along the edge of the sports ground, and make for the woods at the foot of Piz Rosatsch. The path begins here, heading left along the edge of the woods before veering right to enter a narrow valley with a stream easing through it. The path goes through this valley and leads directly to the huddle of alp huts overlooking the pastures of Alp da Staz. Drop down to cross the pasture. Go over the stream and enter the woods ahead. The path wanders through to reach the sunny glade in which the tarn of Stazersee gleams in its delectable setting. Follow the broad track towards St. Moritz, but leave it when the opportunity arises, to go down to the lakeside and head right along the edge of the Lake of St. Moritz back to the town.

VAL BERNINA

Position: Running south-east from the flood-plain of the Upper Engadine below St. Moritz, and stretching for 18 kilometres to the head of the Bernina Pass.

Maps: Landeskarte der Schweiz 1:50,000 series Nos.268 'Julier Pass' and 269 'Bernina Pass' 1:100,000 series No.44 'Maloja Pass' Kümmerly and Frey 'Wanderkarte-Oberengadin' 1:50,000

Valley Base: Pontresina (1,805m)

Huts: Coaz Hut (2,610m), Tschierva Hut (2,573m), Boval Hut (2,495m), Berghaus Diavolezza (2,973m), Georgyhütte (3,176m)

Val Bernina is a much more narrow trench than parts of the Engadine Lakes area, but being on the very edge of the snow and ice peaks of the Bernina Alps, it has enormous appeal. From the main valley two side glens carve away to the south; the Roseg and Morteratsch Valleys. They are glaciated glens with big mountains soaring above them, gleaming in the sun, their snowfields holding permanent winter, their ice sheets grinding away at the mountainsides, carving out the steep walls, the shapely ridges, the jagged peaks.

The north side of the valley rises in a wall of green and grey

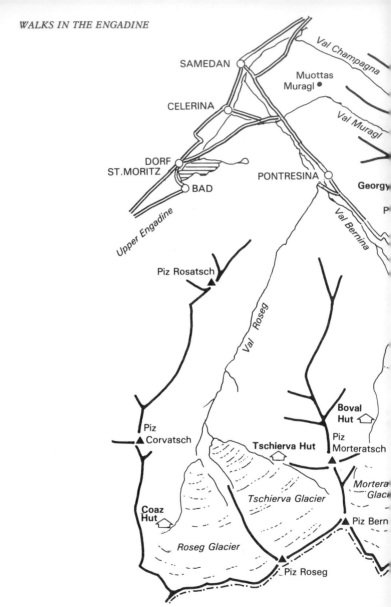

VAL BERNINA

Piz Vadret

z uragl

ard

Albris ▲

Val Prüna

Val dal Fain

Piz Minor ▲

Val Minor

Piz Lagalb ▲

BERNINA PASS

ause ezza

Pers Glacier

Cambrena Glacier

Lago Bianco

Piz Palü ▲

ö

N

SCALE

0   5 kms

mountain. There are side glens here, too, but they have lost their glaciers. Instead, pastures are rich with flowers and streams. On the heights not only chamois are to be seen, but ibex, too; extinct in Switzerland at the turn of the century, but thriving now in their protective state, although shy and often hard to find. If they are to be seen it will be here, on Piz Languard or Piz Albris.

Towards the head of the valley, near the Bernina Pass, there is a certain bleakness about the scene. There are no trees, and the grass wears an almost khaki touch of autumn throughout spring and summer. Spring comes late here. The head of the Bernina Pass is as high as .2,328 metres; the railway reaches 2,253 metres before dropping down into Val Poschiavo, and the footpath runs at about the same height. You can stand knee-deep in snow here in May and gaze down into the Val Poschiavo to see spring in the meadows and the peardrop of a lake dazzling a Mediterranean blue more than thirteen hundred metres below, while Lago Bianco is still hidden under ice beside you. At such times the Poschiavo Valley grows even more appealing than normal; but elsewhere in the Val Bernina there is much to bring pleasure to both the walker and the seeker of alpine flowers.

Route 48:   Pontresina (1,805m) - Hotel-Restaurant Roseg (1,999m)

Grade: 1
Distance: 6.5 kilometres
Height gain: 194 metres
Time: 1½ hours

The Val Roseg stretches into the western edge of the Bernina Alps almost directly opposite Pontresina, so that from many vantage points along the main shopping street, one gains a clear view of the valley's splendour. It is a green and pleasant valley, wooded for much of the way, but then giving out to a glacial plain with snow and icefields at its head, and with many lovely white peaks forming the southern boundary; Piz Sella, Dschimels, Glüschaint, Muongia, Il Chapüt- schin. But best of all, as you go deeper into the valley, the great crusty fang of Piz Roseg. This walk is probably the most popular outing from Pontresina. Rarely will it be walked in solitude, but the valley is long enough to enable one to settle to a gentle pace and wander in peace. It is lovely in every season, and it doesn't matter whether you walk along it in full summer or swish through on *langlauf* skis in winter; whether you explore it for the first time or the twentieth, there is always something new to see and to enjoy.

In June the meadows are alive with flowers. In October the larches form a golden avenue through which to walk. There are red squirrels among the trees, chamois on the slopes above the woods, and marmots in the glacial plain near the hotel. And always splendid views.

Cross from Pontresina town centre to the railway station beyond the bypass road. Just before the station approach road bears round to the right, another road goes straight ahead to enter Val Roseg. Please note: motor vehicles are forbidden in this valley (except delivery vehicles serving the hotel) and the only traffic likely to be met will be horse-drawn carriages, acting as taxis on hire from the road approaching the valley near the station.

Go over the railway line and follow the track all the way through Val Roseg. There is a footpath which runs along the far side of the river, but it is better to go up-valley one way and return by the alternative route. For some time the track gradually gains height with the river below to the left, but after a while you cross to the eastern side and continue until suddenly the valley opens out and there's a stony glacial plain ahead. The track now bears round to the right, crossing the river again, and reaches the Hotel-Restaurant Roseg at the foot of the Fuorcla Surlej path. For a clearer view of Piz Roseg and Bernina, continue along the valley beyond the hotel on a path used as the approach route to the Coaz hut. A short distance along this even more impressive views are to be enjoyed.

Route 49: Pontresina (1,805m) - Val Roseg - Coaz Hut (2,610m)

Grade: 2
Distance: 13.5 kilometres
Height gain: 805 metres
Time: 4-4½ hours

The Coaz Hut is an attractive sixteen-sided building designed by the specialist, Jakob Echenmoser, and opened in 1964 to replace an earlier hut. It occupies a perch of rock known as 'Plattas', overlooking the Roseg Glacier, and enjoys splendid views of icefield and mountain and the valley pouring away to the north. It has room for 55 in its dormitories, and there's a guardian in residence from the end of June until the end of September, at which times there are meals and drinks available. The path to it introduces the walker to the world of high mountain scenery with dramatic effect, and the crevasse-ridden turmoil of the glacier nearby contrasts markedly with the soft and luxurious wood-and-pasture country of the lower Val Roseg.

Take Route 48 as far as the hotel. Then, ignoring the path which climbs the hillside to Fuorcla Surlej, continue in the same direction along the valley on the other path. Where it forks take the right-hand trail sloping up the hillside to reach the buildings of Alp Ota (2,257m). Continue to climb along the path, gaining height without difficulty and enjoying the magnificent scenery displayed before you. The path then starts to contour along the hillside. Eventually the hut comes into sight. Shortly after, the path is joined by another coming from the left, and in a few more minutes the hut is reached.

Route 50: Pontresina (1,805m) - Val Roseg - Tschierva Hut (2,573m)

Grade: 2
Distance: 11.5 kilometres
Height gain: 768 metres
Time: 3½ hours

Many of the finest ice climbs in the Bernina range are accessible from the Tschierva hut, in addition to a number of classic standards on peaks like Piz Bernina, Piz Morteratsch, Scerscen and Roseg. As a consequence, it's a popular hut and likely to be crowded during the main weeks of summer. It is built on the moraine wall of the Tschierva Glacier with a magnificent panorama of high peaks and tumbling icefalls. Enlarged in 1970 to accommodate 100 people, it has a guardian in residence from June until October, offering a full meals service in dramatic surroundings.

Take Route 48 as far as the bridge which leads across the northern end of the glacial plain to the hotel-restaurant. Instead of crossing this, continue along the path which heads up-valley on its left-hand side. Go through the flower-decked pastures of Alp Misaun, rise among trees and shortly after, the trail begins to climb away from the sparse larch and pine slopes towards the moraine bordering the Tschierva Glacier. Keep alert for signs of marmots. Walking up here one June morning I watched a pair newly-emerged from hibernation playing on the path directly in front of me. For several minutes I sat watching them before they became aware of my presence and raced away to their burrows. There are also chamois on the slopes near the hut.

The path zig-zags away from the huts of Alp Margun-Misaun (2,245m), gaining height with views growing all around. Then through a gully between the hillside and moraine of the glacier, before making the final climb up to the Tschierva hut overlooking a wild turmoil of ice.

The Morteratsch Valley, Boval Hut route 52, with Piz Palü and Bellavista

Route 51:   Coaz Hut (2,610m) - Tschierva Hut (2,573m)

Grade: 2
Distance: 12 kilometres
Height gain: 579 metres   Height loss: 616 metres
Time: 3 hours

The normal route linking these two huts combines the approach paths desribed above. First descend to the Hotel-Restaurant Roseg from the Coaz Hut by reversing Route 49, and continue along the track across the valley to reach the bridge. Over this turn right and follow the path described in Route 50 above. (Coaz to Hotel Roseg: 1½ hours. Hotel Roseg to Tschierva Hut: 1½ hours.)

Route 52:   Pontresina (1,805m) - Morteratsch - Boval Hut (2,495m)

Grade: 2
Distance: 10.5 kilometres

Height gain: 690 metres
Time: 3½ hours

After wandering through Val Roseg, the next most popular excursion from Pontresina must surely be this one along the edge of the Morteratsch Glacier to the Boval Hut. It is understandably popular, for it is a walk with spectacular high mountain scenery luring the walker on, from fragrant pine and larch woods to the great snow and ice giants of Piz Palü, Bellavista and Piz Bernina; a panorama of considerable character and beauty, seen from an easy-graded path and with prospects of refreshment at the hut, set as it is with the dazzling peaks spread out before you.

The Boval Hut is one of Switzerland's busiest. It has room for 100 in its dormitories, with a guardian in residence between the middle of March and October. Meals and drinks are available to casual visitors as well as to overnight residents.

One of the dominant features of this walk is the presence of the Morteratsch Glacier. It is formed high on the peaks ahead where the accumulated snows press down to create huge depths of ice; some of this hanging in enormous billows and cliffs on the faces of the mountains. A little above the Boval Hut the main glacier is joined by another coming from the east. This is the Pers Glacier whose birthplace lies high up on the topmost slopes of Piz Palü. Where the two icefields join forces there stands a rocky island amid the ice; Isla Persa. Then, forging northwards, the swollen glacier noses down the long Morteratsch Valley in an extensive slow-moving river. However, this is now receding, and from the glacial snout down to the valley's entrance, a series of markers indicate the progress of this recession. If you have time after your day's walk, return in the bed of the valley from Morteratsch station to the glacier itself and track the course of this ice river over several decades.

Many who visit the Boval Hut from Pontresina either take the train to Morteratsch station, thereby saving about 1½ hours of walking at the start of the day, or use the train for the homeward journey. The route given here actually begins in Pontresina, crosses the valley towards the entrance of Val Roseg, then follows a path heading left through trees towards the Surovas station. The path walks alongside the railway line for a while, keeping the line between the path and the river. It wanders through pine forests, and then branches away to the right, gaining height to avoid a needless detour to the Morteratsch Hotel and railway station in the mouth of the Morteratsch Valley.

Once you enter the valley there's a marvellous gleam of snow and ice ahead; a view familiar from countless Swiss calendars and chocolate boxes, but being there, within that scenery, is a multi-dimensional experience. There is the fragrance of pine and snow and dust from the path, the taste of glacial air, the sound of distant streams and birds piping among the trees. The views become very real, growing all around you. From higher in the valley you may be able to pick out specks of movement on the topmost ridges, or in the broken faces of the mountains, and check the progress of anonymous climbers treading another world high above.

The path is so well-defined it requires no detailed description. It works its way steadily up the western side of the valley along the lateral moraine created by the Morteratsch Glacier. Finally it bears right and climbs the last short slope to the hut.

Route 53:   Pontresina (Diavolezza Cableway) (2,093m) - Berghaus Diavolezza (2,973m)

Grade: 2
Distance: 5 kilometres
Height gain: 880 metres
Time: 3 hours

Practically every walk in this book is designed to make the most of the scenic pleasures of the region; they either lead to specific viewpoints, or wander through an area with delightful vistas to enjoy. But the panorama from Berghaus Diavolezza is one of the finest of them all. It's a view that encompasses the great triple-buttressed ice-gem of Piz Palü; that stretches over Bellavista to Piz Bernina and Piz Morteratsch, with glaciers cascading in waves of ice and snow, motionless, caught as if in a single frame of a movie film, trapped for all time in impossible gestures. Be there early in the morning to catch the red dye of sunrise melting the snows to a rose wash. Or in the evening when shadows distort the icefalls; or at night with stars overhead and a moon dusting the summit snows with its cold lunar beams. It's not bad in the middle of the day, either.

You'll not enjoy the views from Diavolezza in solitude. It's far too popular, too well-known for that. Besides which, there's a cable-car that will whisk the crowds up from the valley in just ten minutes. The panorama is the same for them as it is for the walker. But how much more will it be appreciated if you've earned it with a stiff walk of three hours?

Either take the train from Pontresina to the Diavolezza station, or drive to the cable-car base. There is a very large car park which is

Bernina and Piz Morteratsch from Diavolezza

filled in winter, and pretty nearly so in summer too. The path begins
here. It leads up the hillside a little to the right of the line of the cable-
car over grassy slopes dotted with shrubs, and winds its way easily to
join another path coming from Bernina Suot, a little way down-valley.
The path becomes a broad track - a ski piste in winter - and this enters
a hanging valley, climbs to its head and emerges to the east near a little
lake. At this point the way divides. The piste track continues round to
the right, while a more narrow path, marked *Sommerweg*, goes left,
crosses a stream flowing from the lake, and climbs onto the shoulder
of Sass Queder. This is the path to take.

It is an interesting, enjoyable ascent on a path that zig-zags steeply
in places, but always with good views down towards Bernina Pass and
the hint of Val Poschiavo below. It crosses a couple of broad snow
patches, then eases to cross the final slope of *névé* beyond which there
is a low stony ridge with Berghaus Diavolezza a short stroll away to the
right.

Diavolezza is a privately-owned enterprise with a large and busy
restaurant. If offers *matratzenlager* accommodation at rates a little
above SAC hut charges, but the food is very good and plentiful, and
the setting could hardly be better.

Route 54:   Diavolezza (2,973m) - Munt Pers (3,207m)

Grade: 2
Distance: 2 kilometres
Height gain: 234 metres
Time: 1¼ hours

Munt Pers is the little summit standing to the north-west of Berghaus Diavolezza, and the panorama it commands is truly spectacular. It gives a 360 degree vista of snow peak and deep green valley. It looks way out to far-off mountains in Switzerland, Austria and Italy, and it is entertaining to attempt to recognise peaks that occupy a distant horizon.

The path to it is easy and well-defined. It leads from the Berghaus along the crest of the ridge, keeping to the left of it, then veers south to avoid the rocks of point 3,141m, before climbing the few zig-zags to the summit of Munt Pers.

Route 55:   Diavolezza (2,973m) - Boval Hut (2,495m)

Grade: 3 (Involves glacier crossing, but guides available.)
Distance: 4.5 kilometres
Height loss: 500 metres
Time: 3 hours

This classic glacier crossing to the Boval hut should not be difficult for those experienced in dealing with icefields and not put off by open crevasses. But the necessary equipment should be used and care always exercised, particularly if the glacier be snow covered. Daily throughout the summer, weather permitting, a guided party leaves Diavolezza for the Boval hut, and for the inexperienced who would like to do this route, it is recommended that they join one of these parties. Make sure you are at Diavolezza by about 11.00 a.m. in order to make arrangements.

A path drops down from the Berghaus to the edge of the Pers Glacier opposite a rocky promontory that separates the Pers from the Morteratsch Glacier. This is the rognon known as Isla Persa, and under normal summer conditions there will be ample tracks across the glacier leading to it. Having reached Isla Persa a narrow path leads over the grassy ledges and down slabs and boulders quite steeply heading west, and dropping down to a moraine bank containing a small tarn. The route skirts this to the south, guided by cairns, and brings you to the edge of the Morteratsch Glacier some short distance

Piz Palü from Diavolezza

south-west of the moraine tarn. Crossing this portion of the glacier should not be unduly difficult under normal conditions, and there will invariably be sufficient markings from previous climbers and trekkers to make a reasonable trail. If not, swing south of west, keeping alert for open crevasses towards the centre of the glacier. Then veer north-westwards to gain the bank, climbing along a path that leads directly to the Boval hut.

Route 56: **Pontresina (Muottas Muragl) (2,453m) - Lej Muragl (2,713m) - Chamanna Segantini (2,731m) - Pontresina (1,805m)**

Grade: 2
Distance: 10.5 kilometres
Height gain: 278 metres   Height loss: 926 metres
Time: 5 hours

A stiff walk through idyllic mountain scenery is on offer with this route. A gentle green valley with a clear tarn at its head makes the initial stroll a fairly relaxing affair, but the return path is suddenly traded for a sharp ascent by way of numerous zig-zags, to a fabulous viewpoint overlooking the Upper Engadine, the Val Roseg and its glaciers and the Bernina group laid out before you. At Chamanna Segantini you can relax with a drink at a spot far above the valley where the painter, Giovanni Segantini, spent the last days of his life, in September 1899. (He is buried in Maloja, and in St. Moritz there is a museum devoted to his work and is well worth a visit.) Leaving the Segantini hut one can either descend by path to Alp Languard, where the chair-lift can then be taken down to Pontresina, or walk all the way down on a steep and winding path.

A little over two kilometres down-valley from Pontresina is Punt Muragl, where a funicular railway climbs up the hillside to Muottas Muragl. Here there is a restaurant and hotel with a glorious view over the Engadine lakes; a noted beauty spot with yet another panorama often depicted on Swiss calendars. There are three main paths leading away from the upper station, but the one to take for Lej Muragl is the central one that goes uphill a little before swinging off to the right to follow just below the line of a ridge running south-eastwards towards the peak of Piz Vadret (3,199m). Walk along this path for about an hour and a half, by which time it drops to the lake's edge. (This path actually continues alongside the lake, then crosses Fuorcla Muragl beyond, to explore Val Prüna.)

Having reached the lake, turn back on the valley path which returns towards Muottas Muragl beside the stream, but after some time another path cuts off to the left and climbs steeply up the hillside by way of many zig-zags to cross the ridge which effectively blocks all views to the south. On topping the ridge a magnificent panorama unfolds before you, and there squats the Segantini hut; a perfect place to rest for a while.

Leaving Chamanna Segantini, descend eastwards on the footpath until it forks. Straight ahead the route leads by a narrow trail to Alp Languard and the chair-lift option down to Pontresina (or, of course, a continuing footpath down from Alp Languard), or take the right fork steeply down to Unterer Schafberg (restaurant) and through the woods to reach Pontresina near the Protestant church. Either way will be a little tiring on the legs. But equally worthwhile.

**Route 57: Pontresina (Muottas Muragl) (2,453m) -
Unterer Schafberg (2,231m) - Alp Languard (2,204m) -
Pontresina (1,805m)**

Grade: 2
Distance: 9.5 kilometres

Height loss: 648 metres
Time: 2½-3 hours

This walk follows the *Hochweg* trail across the hillside way above Pontresina. It is yet another fine scenic route, not too demanding, but very rewarding and one that can just as satisfactorily be walked from Alp Languard chair-lift to Muottas Muragl. (In which case allow an extra half-hour from the top of the chair-lift, or 1¼ hours extra from Pontresina.)

Take the funicular railway from Punt Muragl to Muottas Muragl. On leaving the upper station follow the path to the right, which leads into Val Muragl stretching away to the south-east. In the valley, just above the stream, bear left on reaching another crossing path by a hut and walk up-valley a short distance. On reaching a footbridge over the stream, cross and turn right on the trail that leads round the grassy slopes of Munt da la Bes-cha. This is the so-called *Hochweg*. At once the views are delightful, the path clear and easy to follow.

On reaching Unterer Schafberg, where there is a restaurant, continue south-eastwards directly above Pontresina, so to reach the Alp Languard chair-lift. Follow either of two paths steeply down through the woods to Pontresina.

Route 58:   Pontresina (1,805m) - Piz Languard (3,262m)

Grade: 2-3
Distance: 5 kilometres
Height gain: 1,457 metres
Time: 3½-4 hours

For generations Piz Languard has been recognised as a spectacular viewpoint, almost to the point of being hackneyed. It is also one of the easiest ascents of a mountain over 3,000 metres in this corner of the Alps. The panorama from the summit encompasses all the Bernina group to the south, and the lake region of the Upper Engadine disappearing behind the blocking lump of Piz Rosatsch. Far off in the west the Mischabel peaks above Saas Fee can just be seen; in the north rise the jagged peaks that wall the Lower Engadine; to the north-east, the Wildspitze spears the horizon; in the east Konigspitze and Monte Cristallo stand side by side.

As the sun goes down, the summit snows of Piz Palü, Bellavista and Piz Bernina hold the last pink stain long after the valleys have sunken in the shadow of night, while sunrise seen from this vantage point is a-dazzle of wonder.

Twenty minutes below the summit is perched the privately-owned *Georgyhütte,* an extremely popular overnight resting place offering *matratzenlager* accommodation and meals for those who would catch a memorable sunrise. So popular is it, that reservations will in all likelihood need to be made in advance to ensure bedspace.

Either take the chair-lift from Pontresina to Alp Languard, or follow one or other of the steeply climbing footpaths signposted from the main street. From Alp Languard signs indicate the route to Piz Languard. It heads steadily uphill on the northern slopes above Val Languard, clearly marked and well-used. It enters a nature protection zone, continues to gain height with several alternative paths leading away, and arrives at the Georgyhütte, set on the south-east ridge of the mountain, after about 3¼ hours. Refreshments are available here, whether or not you plan to stay overnight. The views are superb. Continue up the ridge to the summit, which takes about another twenty minutes.

The slopes of Piz Languard are sometimes grazed by ibex, and either evening time or early mornings are the most likely periods to catch sight of them. Very early one morning, shortly after dawn, I was descending the north-west ridge alone when I heard a pair of adult males fighting. And a few moments later found myself surrounded by a herd of more than a dozen of them. Obscured by morning shadow I remained in their presence for nearly half an hour before the sun topped the ridge and exposed the fact that I was not just another ibex. The mountainside was cleared in seconds. But the memory of that morning, their musty smell, their sneezing and grunting, their ragged late-summer coats and their huge sickle-shaped horns, remains with me to this day, many years after the event. Walk quietly and with ears and eyes alert, and you too may be rewarded.

**Route 59: Pontresina (1,805m) - Crasta Languard -
        Fuorcla Pischa (2,874m) - Val da Fain -
        Bernina Suot (2,046m)**

Grade: 3
Distance: 12.5 kilometres
Height gain: 1,069 metres   Height loss: 828 metres
Time: 6 hours

Since the greater part of this route's ascent follows the path to Piz Languard, it could happily be adopted as an alternative way down, going as it does over Languard's south-eastern ridge and dropping via

Val da Fain into the Val Bernina. On the other hand, it is an interesting outing in its own right, and one that gives an opportunity to catch sight of ibex, chamois and marmots, and some lovely alpine plants.

Take Route 58 to a point below the Georgyhütte, just as the tight zig-zags begin. The path divides. Left climbs steeply to Piz Languard, and straight ahead follows below the ridge of Crasta Languard. This path leads airily along to cross through the col of Fuorcla Pischa (3½-4 hours from Pontresina). The region ahead now is a wild and somewhat desolate one; bare rocks, snow patches, tiny arctic pools. But there are also lovely alpine plants to be found among the seemingly lifeless rocks. The path forks, but our route continues ahead (the right-hand of two paths) and works its way to another pass, guided by cairns. This pass is unmarked on the map, but is Fuorcla S-chüdella (2,790m), and it leads out of wilderness to a brighter world. Below lies the Val da Fain, and off to the south, the lovely Bernina mountains once more.

Down grassy hillsides with flowers around, the path descends into the valley where it turns onto a broad track on the right bank of a lively stream, passes Alp Bernina on the far side of the stream, and emerges into the Val Bernina with the Diavolezza cableway rising opposite. Turn right in the valley and walk along to Bernina Suot railway station for the train back to Pontresina.

Route 60: Pontresina (1,805m) - Fuorcla Pischa (2,874m) -
Fuorcla Prüna (2,836m) - Alp Prüna (2,270m) -
Val Chamuera - La Punt (1,687m)

Grade: 3
Distance: 22 kilometres
Height gain: 1,069 metres   Height loss: 1,187 metres
Time: 7½-8 hours

A hard day's walking, but one that explores some of the lesser-known valleys of the Engadine region after crossing two high passes and traversing a wild patch of countryside. If this route is considered too long for one day, consider spending a night at the Georgyhütte on Piz Languard, catch sunrise from the summit, then spend the remainder of the day wandering this path.

Take Route 59 from Pontresina over Fuorcla Pischa. On the eastern side of the pass, bear left where the path forks, traverse the slope and cross through Fuorcla Prüna. Just below this pass lie a couple of tarns. Pass these to the left and go round a rocky bluff before descending northwards into the head of Val Prüna along a marked trail. The way crosses the stream flowing through the valley on two or three occasions, is joined by another path coming from the left (over Fuorcla Muragl - see Route 56) and reaches Alp Prüna. North of the alp continue to lose height gradually, bearing left away from the stream just before coming to the junction with Val Chamuera at Serlas. Cross the main Chamuera stream onto its right bank where you will join another track. Head left, ignoring another trail which forks off to the right, and walk down the length of Val Chamuera, soon among trees, on the right bank of the stream all the way. On emerging into the Engadine at Chamues-ch, cross the valley by road to La Punt (or Madulain if preferred) for the train back to Pontresina via Samedan.

Route 61: Pontresina (Alp Languard) (2,201m) - Chamanna Paradis (2,540m)

Grade: 2
Distance: 2 kilometres
Height gain: 339 metres
Time: 1 hour

Given just half a day in which to spend time in relaxing surroundings and with a pleasant view, this short trip is worth considering. Perhaps you must leave for home in the afternoon and feel the need to spend a brief period in the morning for one last look at the mountains; or perhaps the weather has been bad during the morning and it clears at mid-day - then this outing will bring a breath of fresh air.

Take the chair-lift to Alp Languard and from there choose one of two paths. One leads by a series of zig-zags from the stream below the alp, straight up the crest of the ridge opposite to reach the Paradis restaurant by the most direct route. The alternative is to follow the trail into Val Languard which cuts away to the east, then branch off to the right at the first footpath, cross the stream and go up to the minor grassy ridge, then bear left to find Chamanna Paradis. Views here gaze out directly to the south along the Morteratsch Glacier to the Bernina group beyond. A lovely spot.

Other Routes in Val Bernina:

There will be no shortage of ideas for additional outings in Val Bernina and the surrounding area. A glance at the map will illustrate numerous possibilities. Towards the head of the valley, for example, there is a walk through **Val da Fain** as far as the Italian border at Fuorcla la

Stretta; or alternatively branch away from the valley at Alp la Stretta and climb northwards over the mountains and descend into the head-waters of Val Chamuera.

A little to the east of Val da Fain there's **Val Minor** which makes a moat to the north of Piz Lagalb. An easy walk up-valley to Lej Minor is worth a morning's exercise; while having taken the cable-car onto the summit of **Piz Lagalb**, where the extensive views are glorious, there are several paths down, some of considerable interest to botanists. There is also a circuit of Piz Lagalb made possible by linking the valleys by way of easy passes.

From the **Bernina Pass** there are footpaths that lead down to lovely Alp Grüm, or to Alp Palü with its tarn - two good places to find alpine flowers; or all the way down into the Val Poschiavo; or across to the green luxury of **Val da Camp** with its woods and pastures and little lakes.

No shortage of ideas, indeed. Having exhausted all the possibilities in this book, it will be time to dream up excursions of your own. There are sufficient variations to last a lifetime.

UPPER ENGADINE - NORHTERN REGION (CELERINA TO CINUOS-CHEL)

Position:	Stretching north-eastwards from below St. Moritz to the Lower Engadine's limits just north of Val Susauna.
Maps:	Landeskarte der Schweiz 1:50,000 series Nos.268 'Julier Pass', 258 'Bergün' and 259 'Ofenpass' 1:100,000 series Nos.44 'Maloja Pass' and 39 'Flüela Pass' Kümmerly and Frey 'Wanderkarte-Oberengadin' 1:50,000
Valley Bases:	Celerina (1,724m), Samedan (1,720m), Bever (1,708m), Zuoz (1,716m)
Huts:	Jürg Jenatsch Hut (2,652m), Es-cha Hut (2,594m), Kesch Hut (2,632m)

Below the wooded sill of St. Moritz Dorf the Engadine suddenly loses height, but it broadens in the flat plain where Val Bernina flows in from the right, soon to narrow once more towards Bever. Here the valley takes on a different appearance; it runs in a straight shaft between mountains that fold away on either side to allow lateral valleys to feed in. These mountains conform to a general rule of orderliness.

They are wooded to almost waist-height, then grassy slopes lead up to bare crowns. There's little permanent snow on them, no lengthy glaciers carving down, no savage corries or bristling ridges or luring walls to tempt the climber. Both mountain and valley alike show a gentle face, but they are certainly not without their charms.

The valley floor is mostly flat, and the Inn has been contained within its bed by concrete walls to hold back the threat of flooding. The land is fertile, side valleys lush and welcome and rich in greenery. In these valleys the walker will experience a far greater sense of solitude and isolation than may be found higher in the Engadine, for this is a comparatively neglected region. It need not be so, for there is much to be said for it, and it offers a welcome interlude between Upper Engadine extravagance and Lower Engadine tradition; a halfway house between two immediately attractive regions.

Route 62:   Celerina (1,724m) - Samedan (Selvas-Plaunas) (1,848m) - Bever (1,708m)

Grade: 1-2
Distance: 10.5 kilometres
Height gain: 124 metres   Height loss: 140 metres
Time: 3 hours

A hillside walk linking three villages, it passes through one of the Engadine's many plant protection zones. Walked in the early summer, the meadows are bright with flowers, the clanging of cow bells loud in your ears, the views stretching down the valley as through an open tunnel. Above Celerina the hillsides are adorned with ski tows, and there's a gondola lift swinging above the woods into Val Saluver where, at Marguns, the valley has been sacrificed to the ski industry. This walk keeps below most of that.

Choose a path from the village up onto the hillsides above, and bear right among trees into the early reaches of Val Saluver. Cross the stream by some buildings and bear right along the northern slopes and then take the second path heading off to the left as you round the hillside. This will lead along the edge of larch woods to Christolais (1,846m) at a junction of several paths. Take that which goes straight ahead, continuing to contour along the hillside. It skirts above Samedan village, continues on, enters more woods and swings into the Val Bever opening, heading left. The trail comes level with the railway, crosses it and the river, and turns right to go along the hillside before dropping into Bever. From this village take either train or Postbus back to Celerina.

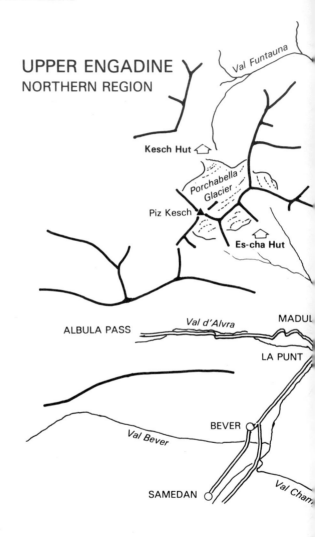

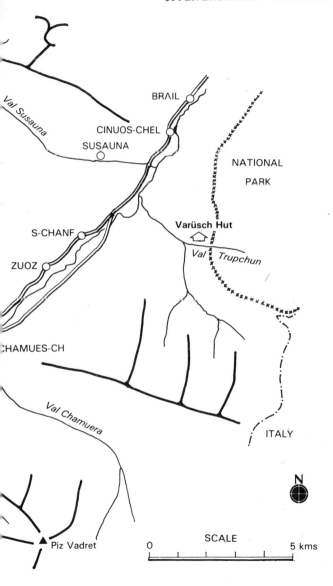

BRAIL

CINUOS-CHEL

SUSAUNA

Val Susauna

NATIONAL

PARK

Varüsch Hut

Val Trupchun

S-CHANF

ZUOZ

CHAMUES-CH

Val Chamuera

ITALY

Piz Vadret

N

SCALE

0   5 kms

111

Route 63: **Samedan (1,720m) - Val Champagna -**
Fuorcla Val Champagna (2,803m) - Lej Muragl (2,713m)
Muottas Muragl (2,453m)

Grade: 2-3
Distance: 12 kilometres
Height gain: 1,083 metres   Height loss: 350 metres
Time: 4½ hours

Val Champagna is one of those little-visited valleys tucked away from
the popular resorts and with no particular feature to draw the walker
into its recesses. Thus we have one of the best reasons for tackling this
route. It leads through this tight, narrow, steeply-climbing valley to its
head below the crags of Piz Vadret, then crosses its southern wall to
descend a better-known footpath to the fleshpots of the Muottas
Muragl restaurant and funicular railway leading down to the junction
of Val Bernina with the Engadine.

From the road below Samedan take the footpath which heads down-
valley on the left bank of the river, and cross to the right bank at a
bridge which will take you to the edge of Samedan airfield. Head
north to go round the far end of the runway, then bear right to the
woods of Chuoz in the mouth of Val Champagna. Take the path leading into the valley, cross the stream and follow it along its true left
bank (right-hand side as you ascend the valley). The path is clear for
most of the way, but it climbs at a good angle as the valley steepens. It
then recrosses to the northern side of the stream and goes up to the
lonely hut of Alp Champagna (2,371m).

Above Alp Champagna the path deteriorates, but the way continues
above the stream on the north side, still gaining height with Piz Vadret
looming overhead. At the head of the stream cross over to the south
and make for the saddle of Fuorcla Val Champagna, through which
you emerge above the tarn of Lej Muragl. Drop down now towards
the lake's western end and join the path coming from Muottas
Muragl. This leads directly to the restaurant and funicular station
with its superb open views over the Upper Engadine's lakes; a marked
contrast with the constricted views of Val Champagna.

Route 64: **Samedan (1,720m) - Muottas Muragl (2,453m) -**
Lej Muragl (2,713m) - Fuorcla Val Champagna (2,803m)
Val Champagna - Samedan

Grade: 3
Distance: 16 kilometres

Height gain: 1,083 metres   Height loss: 1,083 metres
Time: 5½ hours

This offering is a variation of Route 63, but instead of ascending through Val Champagna, it descends into it after having first climbed up the shoulder of Muottas Muragl. Sometimes one will be wandering up this initial path with gliders circling overhead, for Samedan airfield is used not only for light aircraft traffic, but also for the towing of gliders. On the ascent of Muottas Muragl there will be the superb Engadine panoramas to enjoy for much of the way too.

Follow Route 63 to the entrance of Val Champagna at Chuoz, but then branch away from the main valley path and take the right fork to climb in tight zig-zags among the trees up the shoulder of the mountain, heading a little east of south. On the ascent through the trees there are alternative paths branching off to the right and left. Ignore these and continue to gain height, coming above the woods to enjoy the spreading views before eventually wandering round the mountainside to reach the funicular and restaurant of Muottas Muragl.

Now take the higher of two paths stretching ahead into Val Muragl. This path follows just below the crest of the left-hand ridge, and comes in about an hour to a point above the little Lej Muragl. Bear left and pass through Fuorcla Val Champagna to the head of Val Champagna below the rough face of Piz Vadret. The way now crosses the head of the valley in a descent to the stream, and goes down along its right-hand side. Shortly after passing the isolated Alp Champagna on its perch, cross to the left bank of the stream on a path that becomes clearer as you lose height. On reaching the mouth of the valley, return to Samedan by the same path as that used at the beginning of the walk.

Route 65:   Bever (1,708m) - Val Bever - Jürg Jenatsch Hut (2,652m)

Grade: 2
Distance: 16 kilometres
Height gain: 944 metres
Time: 4½-5 hours

The approach to the *Chamanna Jenatsch* from Bever leads entirely through the pleasant Val Bever, from its wood-guarded discharge into the Engadine, to its stony head in a little cirque of forgotten mountains. A fairly long walk, it has much to commend it; not least because it is one of the lesser-known corners of the Engadine whose peaks and pastures are unspectacular yet charming. The hut itself can accommodate 60 in its dormitories. There is a guardian at Easter, Whitsun and in July and August. Meals are only provided if booked in advance. Climbs are to be had on neighbouring peaks like Piz Err, Piz Calderas and Piz Jenatsch, and rough walking tours could be devised to lead over craggy passes that are practically unknown to British hillwalkers.

Take either of two tracks out of Bever that lead into the valley cutting away behind the village. They join forces after about a kilometre and follow the river along the right-hand side (true left bank) passing several farms. The railway to Chur disappears into a tunnel at the station of Spinas, one hour from Bever, and it should be noted that for those who may wish to do so, it is possible to take the train from Bever to Spinas in order to reduce walking time. The way continues up-valley, having crossed above the tunnel, still beside trees and still with the river flowing past on the left. Near the junction with the valley of Suvretta da Samedan, seen coming from the south, the path crosses the river to Alp Suvretta. Another path cuts away to the left here. Ignore this and recross to the right-hand side of the river.

The way continues upstream, steadily gaining height as the valley grows a little more wild and the mountains crowd into a blocking amphitheatre ahead, with small glaciers and snowfields cupped in their high corries. Suddenly the path deserts the stream and climbs uphill in a loop or two to bring you direct to the hut. Above lies the icesheet of the little Calderas Glacier, while other snowfields and glacial scarves adorn neighbouring peaks.

Route 66: Bever (1,708m) - Val Bever -
Fuorcla Crap Alv (2,466m) - Albula Pass
(Pass d'Alvra) (2,312m) - La Punt (1,697m)

Grade: 3
Distance: 19 kilometres
Height gain: 758 metres   Height loss: 769 metres
Time: 5½ hours

Val Bever is walled on its northern side by a long ridge of mountains extending westward from Crasta Mora above the village of Bever. On the northern side of this ridge is the Albula road pass linking the Engadine with the splendid valley of Bergün. This walk leads over the ridge by way of Fuorcla Crap Alv, catches a glimpse of Bergün's pasturelands folding neatly over steep mountainsides, and returns to the Engadine roughly following the course of the Albula road.

Take Route 65 from Bever to Spinas station, and continue along Val Bever for perhaps another hour until you come to a path branching off to the right. This climbs the hillside in a series of zig-zags heading west to find the breach of Fuorcla Crap Alv hidden by the crags of the ridge. The route leads through to the northern side and skirts the crags that here form something of a wall, then bears half-right to pass a couple of little tarns. The way divides. Take the right fork and descend in a traverse to the road below the Albula Pass. Cross the road and walk uphill on a path that leads to the Albula Hospice.

Cross to the right-hand side of the road and cut across the open hillside, passing along the southern side of the chilly-looking lake, and follow the course of the road. But when the road crosses to the left-bank of a stream, keep to the right bank, walk on until you reach Alp Nova, and descend on a path all the way into the Engadine, which you'll reach at La Punt.

Route 67:   La Punt (1,697m) - Val Chamuera - Serlas (2,017m)

Grade: 2
Distance: 7.5 kilometres
Height gain: 320 metres
Time: 2 hours

This is a gentle valley walk to an alp at a junction of several paths that lead over high passes. Much of the walk is among woods with green meadows rising out of them, and rocky crests leading to bigger peaks wearing small snowfields and miniature glaciers.

Cross the valley from La Punt to Chamues-ch in the mouth of Val Chamuera. A road links the two communities. Take the track which cuts behind Chamues-ch alongside the Ova Chamuera stream that has woods on either side, and follow this through the valley, gaining height painlessly with a few twists of the track. After some time you emerge from the woods to open hillsides, the stream dashing down to your right, the valley being split ahead. A stream comes down from Val Lavirun through a tight gorge on your left, with the little alp of Acla Veglia below it, and a short distance beyond this you come to the junction of trails at Serlas. One branches left and climbs into Val Lavirun; one crosses the stream and enters Val Prüna opposite, while the main trail continues up-valley before forking over two separate passes.

Route 68:   Madulain (1,697m) - Es-cha Hut (2,594m)

Grade: 2-3
Distance: 6 kilometres
Height gain: 897 metres
Time: 2½-3 hours

North of the Bernina peaks, Piz Kesch is probably the Upper Engadine's most popular mountain with climbers. The peak is 3,417 metres high; a shapely point above steep ridges, and with a broad glacier draped down its northern slopes, and an eastern corrie containing the little Vadret d'Es-cha (Es-cha Glacier). On its south-eastern slopes there sits the comfortable Chamanna Es-cha on a spur of mountain that effectively separates the steep Val Müra from that of Val d'Es-cha. The hut can sleep 40; it has a guardian from the end of June until the beginning of October, and during this period meals and drinks are available. This route could make a pleasant day out; a morning spent wandering up to the hut, lunch there in peaceful surroundings, and a steep afternoon's stroll back to the valley.

Down-valley a little from the centre of Madulain, a track crosses the railway and winds in long loops up the green hillside above the village. It goes through patches of pine and larch wood - has other tracks leading from it to either side, which must be ignored - and bears left into the knuckle fold of Val d'Es-cha whose stream is running below the path. After passing Alp Es-cha Dadour, two paths branch off to the right; one leads along the hillside towards Zuoz, the other climbs up to the vantage point of Alp Belvair. Both should be ignored, but a little farther along the valley the path makes a distinct fork. Here take the right trail to climb steeply north-westwards into the cut of Val Müra. The trail eventually crosses the Müra stream and engages a steep zig-zag pull up the spur of mountainside to reach the Es-cha hut. A fine place for a picnic with Piz Kesch rising enticingly behind.

Outings from the Es-cha Hut:
There are several outing to be made from here, other than the obvious ones that entail climbing peaks. Experienced alpine trekkers could cross the high Porta d'Es-cha (3,008m) and descend the Porchabella Glacier to the **Kesch Hut**, and from there head west down to Alp digl Chant, up the Val Plazbi and over Fuorcla Pischa back to the Es-cha hut, thereby making an effective circuit of Piz Kesch. Alternatively, there's another trek for experienced mountain walkers that goes west, over Fuorcla Pischa and into the head of Val Plazbi, then climbs up to Tschimas da Tisch and follows the crest along to the summit of Piz

Darlux, followed by a sharp descent into **Val Tuors** which in turn leads out to Bergün, where a train could be caught back to the Engadine again. These, and variations of these themes, could make good use of a day or two based on the Es-cha hut. On the other hand, try Route 69 below, for an interesting day's round-trip.

Route 69: Madulain (1,697m) - Es-cha Hut (2,594m) - Gualdauna (2,480m) - Alp Nova (2,114m) - Madulain

Grade: 2-3
Distance: 14.5 kilometres
Height gain: 897 metres   Height loss: 897 metres
Time: 5½-6 hours

For those going up to the Es-cha hut simply for a visit, this route offers an alternative descent, thus creating a fine round-trip. Take Route 68 from Madulain to the hut, continue behind it and fork left on a traversing path that contours round the mountainside to the south. Below, the Val d'Es-cha curves towards the main valley. Above, the mountains mould themselves into spurs and clefts, while beyond the Ova Pischa stream the path leads round the shoulder of mountain to the saddle of Gualdauna, west of point 2,605 metres. Now the path slants down the hillside towards the Albula Pass road. Cut away where convenient to reach the road, cross it and the stream and make for Alp Nova seen below the road. There is a path leading from Alp Nova down into the Engadine. Follow this until it meets the road again at a sharp hairpin bend. Leave the path, walk along the road to its next, upper, hairpin, and then branch away north-eastwards on another path leading across the hillside, through trees and down to Madulain.

Route 70: Zuoz (1,716m) - Inn River - Punt Muragl (1,738m)

Grade: 1
Distance: 14 kilometres
Time: 4 hours

A valley walk all the way, this route follows the River Inn up-valley through flat meadowlands away from the villages that are all reasonably accessible should you decide at any stage to foreshorten the walk. The path is easy and there are no sudden uphill stages to contend with. A leisurely stroll through a landscape of green, with Piz de la

Margna beckoning far away at the head of the valley.

From the station at Zuoz take the road leading down to the river, cross it and the new road beyond, and immediately turn right at the farm called Resgia to follow a track leading a short distance from the Inn. Keep with the river to pass below Madulain, then cut across to meet the bridge that carries a road from La Punt to Chamues-ch. La Punt is on the far side of the river, while Chamues-ch lines the road at the mouth of Val Chamuera to the left. On reaching the road, go between some houses, cross a stream flowing from Val Chamuera and follow the path along the bank of the Inn, still heading upstream.

Opposite Bever the path deserts the river in a brief curve towards the woods, then you have a choice to make. Either stay with the woods to follow their edge southwards, crossing the entrance to Val Champagna, and about 1.5 kilometres farther on branch off into the trees to curve round the lump of hillside forming the boundary of Val Bernina, so to reach Punt Muragl. Or alternatively, go along the edge of Samedan airfield, head back to the river and then walk beside the railway line, or the river beyond it, as far as Punt Muragl. Either way is acceptable. From Punt Muragl, at the foot of the Muottas Muragl funicular, trains will take you back to Zuoz.

Route 71: Zuoz (1,716m) - Acla Laret (2,006m) - Alp Griatschouls (2,165m) - Susauna (1,682m) - Cinuos-chel (1,613m)

Grade: 2
Distance: 9 kilometres
Height gain: 449 metres   Height loss: 552 metres
Time: 4 hours

A hillside, forest and valley walk of considerable charm, this route makes a good introduction to the lovely Val Susauna. The route described takes you to the station at Cinuos-chel - Brail to enable a return to be made to Zuoz, but holders of YHA membership cards might consider spending a night at the spartan, yet utterly delightful, Val Susauna Jugendherberge. Such an arrangement would make a most satisfactory ending to a day's walk, and encourage further inspection of the valley.

From Zuoz village square, with its fountain displaying the bear emblem of the Planta family, follow directions to the Lyceum, then head right along a footpath which climbs the hillside meadows towards pine and larch woods to gain Acla Laret's lonely outpost after almost an hour. From here take the left-hand, uphill, path that goes in long sweeps through forest, then out to open hillside again, so to reach Alp Griatschouls with its fine views down the valley and across to the National Park. Rounding the hillside heading north, the way loses height quite steeply as it descends into Val Susauna, in and out of the tree-clothed slopes. On reaching the valley floor, turn right along a broad track with splendid soft views ahead, and walk on down to the huddle of farms that make up the hamlet of Susauna. The Youth Hostel is the last building, backing onto meadowland.

The track forks near the church. It offers alternative ways down to the Engadine, both of which follow the river and meet at the valley entrance. Here turn left and walk down the road to find Cinuos-chel - Brail railway station.

Route 72:   Susauna (1,682m) - Alp Pignaint (1,873m)

Grade: 1
Distance: 4.5 kilometres
Height gain: 191 metres
Time: 1 hour

This very short stroll is included to illustrate the pleasures that can be won by simply wandering through a soft valley, with gentle pastures, fine trees and a lovely stream running clear. The route follows a broad dirt track all the way. There are no lakes, no dramatic waterfalls, no great glaciers or snowfields, nor particularly shapely mountains to gaze at. Within a region as outstandingly scenic as the Engadine undoubtedly is, Val Susauna has little of immediate impact. Or so it might seem. It remains, however, one of my firm favourites, and one that I could never grow tired of. Try it for yourself and let the special flavour of the valley soak in.

As has already been stated, there is a Youth Hostel in Susauna hamlet. There is also a campsite near the entrance to the valley. From the Engadine road it is possible to drive through the initial two kilometres of Val Susauna on an unmade road that crosses to the left side of the valley and follows the river upstream. Only permit holders may drive into the village of Susauna and beyond, but immediately before you come to the bridge which leads over the river to the community, there is a rough lay-by on the left of the track. Cars may be parked here.

Walk along the track, over the bridge and into Susauna hamlet with its clustered farms and neat little church. Continue up-valley on the

119

Val Susauna Youth Hostel

track all the way. It crosses the Vallember stream a couple of times, leads through pastures and woodlands, with shrubs beside the track and flowers in the grass. Look out for deer and chamois. After some time the track winds uphill with the stream below on the left, then tops a rise and eases down the other side, and the buildings of Alp Pignaint are seen on the far side of the stream below the opening of Val Viluoch. There is a wooden bridge over the stream, and pastures stretching ahead. An unremarkable, yet charming scene. Anywhere along the streamside would make an idyllic site for a picnic.

Route 73: Susauna (1,682m) - Alp Funtauna (2,192m) - Val Funtauna - Kesch Hut (2,632m)

Grade:	2-3
Distance:	12.5 kilometres
Height gain:	950 metres
Time:	3½-4 hours

There are plenty of contrasts on this hut approach, for it begins in the fragrant luxury of Val Susauna and finishes in a gaunt landscape of rock and ice. The Kesch hut, owned by the Davos Section of the SAC, is well-placed for a number of climbs, and can sleep 80 people (40 in its winter quarters). A guardian is in residence for the three months from July until the end of September, with meals and drinks available.

Follow Route 72 as far as the bridge which leads over the stream to Alp Pignaint. Continue up-valley along the main track with the stream on your left. As the valley narrows, so the route crosses to the left side, goes up a little farther, then returns to the right-hand side. The valley curves left and right and is joined by streams flowing from first, Vallorgia to the right, then from the Scaletta Pass ahead. Shortly after this joining of streams you come to Alp Funtauna, superbly set at the mouth of the Val Funtauna.

Head up Val Funtauna on a path that keeps with the stream, then swings into the upper reaches, here known as Val dal Tschüvel, at the crown of which stands Piz Kesch with its glacier draped before it. The path continues to gain height, then leaves the stream's company to bear right, so reaching the hut soon after.

Other Routes from Susauna:

There are two other notable outings that could be considered for the experienced mountain trekker to attempt, both of which lead from Susauna to Davos. The first follows Route 73 as far as Alp Funtauna,

121

then climbs steeply ahead to cross the 2,606 metres **Scaletta Pass** which leads to the Dischmatal. This, in turn, takes a broad track past numerous farms all the way to Davos Dorf. The other suggestion also goes as far as Alp Funtauna, then heads left into Val Funtauna, but instead of veering left again into Val Tschüvel as on the approach to the Kesch hut, it branches off right into a little valley hiding the **Sertig Pass** (2,739m). Once over this a rough descent is made under the crags of the Augstenhornli to the Kühalptal which is, in fact, the upper sanctuary of the larger valley of Sertig. This will bring you out a little south-west of Davos Platz.

A close study of the map will reveal numerous other ways for the walker to design challenging excursions of his own, using the little hamlet of Susauna as a starting point. But, as has already been stressed, the valley itself is delightful enough on its own to satisfy the tastes of most lovers of gentle mountain scenery. It will certainly repay a visit.

Val Tuoi, with Piz Buin

Lower Engadine

In contrast with the Upper Engadine's snow and ice peaks, its extensive lakes and side valleys that lead to glaciers in a raw mountain scenery, the Lower Engadine *(Engiadina Bassa,* or *Unterengadin)* is a more tranquil region; it has long ago shrugged off its glacial armour and wrapped itself now in a lush green cloak. Green meadows, green forests, green hillsides out of which rise grey peaks. It's a deep river-cut swathe, tended with care and attention to detail, man and nature working in a close partnership so that those who wander through it can sense an unhurried calm. It is a landscape of assurance.

Forests are very much a feature of the region. They form a dense covering to the valley sides; spruce, larch, cembra or arolla pine, and the footpaths that weave through them are wandered in a heady fragrance. But it's not all forest, and the rich flower meadows that carpet natural hillside terraces are magnificent in early summer, and they will delight all who walk among them. Wildlife too is abundant - especially in the National Park whose boundaries are contained within those of the Lower Engadine.

This stretch of the valley is proud of its traditions. The Romansch language is spoken everywhere, and the architecture of its hamlets and villages is a heritage of great beauty handed down through the centuries. Here amid sunny pastures, on hillside ledges or in the bed of the valley set a little above the Inn, ancient communities cluster around a cobble-stoned square whose centre-piece is invariably a gushing fountain that pours non-stop into a water-trough. Houses are romantic dwellings with misshapen stone walls that appear to have become bowed down with the weight of centuries. Their huge arched doors are deep-set and in some cases reached by way of a ramp from the street or alleyway. Their windows are tiny and similarly deep-set with ornate wrought iron grills before them, and superb patterns of *sgraffito* etched in the plaster. Some of the walls are pink-washed; most are plastered white with grey-toned scrolls or geometric shapes forming an edge to doorways and windows and even the wall corners themselves. Now and then you'll discover a house with one wall given over to a pictorial image, sometimes hundreds of years old, others comparatively recent expressions by a plasterer or architect intent on maintaining a unique tradition. So it is that some of the villages here become everyday living art galleries, placed in an unadulterated series of landscapes.

It's fifty-five kilometres from Punt Ota, between Cinuos-chel and Brail, where the Lower Engadine begins, to the point where the Inn deserts Switzerland for Austria below Martina. In those fifty-five kilometres there is a world of soft moulded luxury, lush pastures rising to untroubled peaks; a timelessness that is implanted to the wanderer of its footpaths. There are side valleys in plenty to lead the walker into fresh horizons, and stepped hillsides adorned with villages that have history, art and romance in every building and in every alleyway.

Opposite Val Susauna on the eastern side of the valley, the National Park begins, and between Val Trupchun and Zernez where the Spöl's valley cuts back towards the Ofen Pass and Val Mustair beyond, all the eastern mountains and valleys are under the protection of the Park. Then, from the little flood plain occupied by Zernez, the Engadine veers a little to the north before swinging back again towards the north-east on a course it will maintain as far as the Austrian border. In this section the full flavour of the Lower Engadine is to be experienced. It is here that the loveliest of villages are to be found; Guarda, Ardez, old Scuol down towards the river. Here are the best of the side valleys slicing north to the edge of the Silvretta peaks, but the southern glens, cut between mountains of the Engadine Dolomites, are also well worth exploring. They lead to the northern half of the National Park which here has a curious projecting boundary.

This is certainly a very fine region for walking, with something to suit every taste.

Main Valley Bases:

Zernez (1,472m) is ideally situated in the bed of the valley at the junction of the main Engadine road with that of the Ofen Pass (Pass dal Füorn) beyond which lies the soft Italian-flavoured Val Müstair. The National Park is only a short stroll away, and with regular Postbus and train services, almost every part of the valley can be reached with some ease. It is a small, unpretentious town (or large village) with a number of hotels and *pensions*, and a good campsite at the southern end, reached by way of a timber yard's approach road. There are food stores, chemist, banks and all the usual services. The tourist information office is in the main street, and the National Park House, which is highly recommended for a visit, stands beside the Ofen Pass road a short distance from the centre of the village.

Scuol (1,244m) is the only other main base in the Lower Engadine, in so far as tourist facilities are concerned, and it has as close neighbours the resorts of *Tarasp* (with its lovely castle) and *Vulpera*. Scuol itself is divided into old and new. The original village stands a little lower than the new, and consists of delightful traditional buildings (one of which is now a museum) with some of the most photogenic architecture in the whole valley. The new centre of Scuol cannot compare in architectural grace with the old, but its facilities are in line with other modern Swiss resorts. All the usual facilities and services are there; plenty of shops, banks, hotels, holiday apartments etc. The tourist information office has a very helpful staff. Accommodation prices are a little higher than in some of the smaller villages, but there is a highly recommended campsite on the south side of the river, reached through old Scuol, and conveniently placed for trips into the S-charl valley.

Other Valley Bases:

Although there are only two real tourist bases in the Lower Engadine in which a variety of accommodation and services are available, most of the other villages offer lodgings of one kind or another. Some of these villages are extremely attractive in themselves so that a holiday based there would give a head start. Guarda, for example, is fascinating in style and setting, but both its hotels are three star establishments which might put them beyond the pockets of many walking enthusiasts. On the other hand, it is accessible by Postbus or car, so it is not out of reach from an alternative base. And there is a fine walk through Val Tuoi behind it.

Beginning at the boundary between Upper and Lower Engadine, villages offering accommodation are as follows: *Cinuos-chel*, though small, has one *pension* with twenty beds, and a campsite nearby, opposite the entrance to Val Susauna. On the way to the Ofen Pass out of Zernez, there is a *Naturfreund* hostel at *Ova Spin*, a *matratzenlager* and National Park Hotel at *Il Fuorn*.

Lower in the Engadine beyond Zernez, *Susch* guards the approach to the Flüela Pass. In this little village there are a few hotels and *pensions* and a small campsite. *Lavin* nearby sits directly beneath the lofty pyramid of Piz Linard (3,411m), the highest of the Silvretta group of mountains and seen in profile so well from Zernez. In Lavin there is one 40 bed hotel. *Guarda* has already been mentioned for its classic architectural styles and for its situation, tucked above the main valley road on a shelf of pasture with lovely views across to the Engadine Dolomite peaks. Accommodation facilities are expected to grow with increased demand, although there should be strong protective measures enforced to ensure it retains its essential character. At present there are one or two shops, and limited car parking with access through a narrow alleyway.

Guarda is linked with *Ardez* by a narrow hillside track, but more easily reached by a turning off the main road. This village, like Guarda, has many lovely houses in the traditional style, and looks out across the valley from its own hillside perch. Limited accommodation available, one or two shops of a general nature. *Ftan* is larger and rather more sprawling on its hillside above the valley. At the time of writing this village is expanding and will no doubt increase its complement of hotels beyond the present two. (One 4-star, the other three star.)

S-charl, deep within its valley behind Scuol, has hotels, *pensions* and *matratzenlager* accommodation in a quiet, off-the-beaten-track summer-only village. Beyond Scuol a road branches off left away from the main valley road, and angles up the hillside to reach *Sent,* another village with fine views across the valley, and making the most of its sunny south-facing position. It has two hotels.

Mountain Huts:

There are five huts within the area covered by this section of the guide; three of which are SAC huts, one was built by a commercial organisation but is open to all walkers, and the other belongs to the National Park Authority. Each offers *matratzenlager* accommodation, but not all have meals available.

Starting in the south and working northwards, these huts are as follows: the *Varüsch Hut* (1,736m) in Val Trupchun just outside the National Park's boundary, and *Blockhaus Cluozza* (1,880m) in the heart of the Park, set deep in the Cluozza valley and reached from Zernez in about three hours, or by a fine route from Varüsch in 6½ hours. The Swiss Alpine Club huts are here more simple than those situated in the Bernina and Bregaglia mountains. Below Piz Linard, and reached in about 3 hours from Lavin, is the little *Linard Hut* (2,327m), and at the head of Val Tuoi, directly below Piz Buin and the Dreiländerspitze, is the largest of these huts, the *Tuoi Hut* (2,250m). On the south side of the Lower Engadine, and some 3½ hours from Scuol, is the *Lischana Hut* (2,500m), midway between Piz Lischana and Piz San Jon.

Campanula scheuchzeri

127

LOWER ENGADINE ROUTES

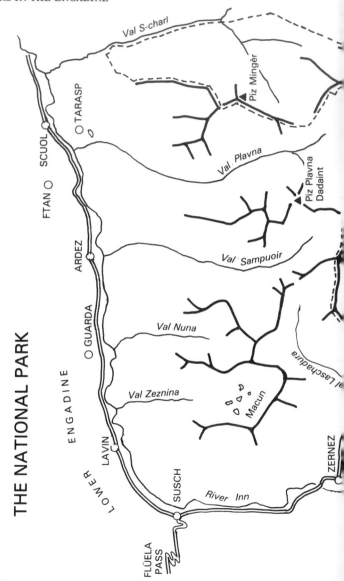

THE NATIONAL PARK

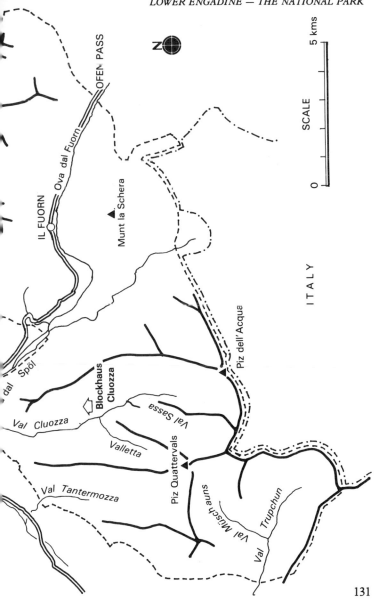

THE NATIONAL PARK

Position:	Contained entirely within the eastern side of the Lower Engadine region, from Val Trupchun in the south-west, to Val S-charl's lower reaches near Scuol in the north-east, and stretching to the Ofen Pass (Pass dal Füorn) which links the Engadine with Val Müstair.
Maps:	Landeskarte der Schweiz 1:50,000 series No.259 'Ofenpass' 1:100,000 series No.39 'Flüela Pass' Kümmerly and Frey 'Wanderkarte-Oberengadin' 1:100,000
Valley Bases:	Zernez (1,472m), Scuol (1,244m), Il Fuorn (Ofen Pass) (1,794m)
Huts:	Varüsch Hut (1,736m), Blockhaus Cluozza (1,880m)

Switzerland has only one National Park, the oldest in Europe, and that is situated well within the area covered by this guide. In many respects it is unique.

It comes as something of a surprise to find that not so very far from the extrovert resorts of St. Moritz and Pontresina, there lies an area of tranquility and modest charm, where Man the intruder plays a very subordinate role to the demands of Nature. But such is the reality of the Park, and the visitor can hardly fail to be impressed by the peculiar atmosphere experienced there. Within its boundaries ramblers may not depart from the authorised paths, nor picnic except in specified places. Visitors must not pick flowers or berries, camp out, disturb the animals, cut wood, leave litter or fish the streams. Such restrictions may seem a touch too authoritarian for some, but since there are few enough places left in Europe that Man has not moulded to his own specific use, it is perhaps no bad thing to allow Nature freedom to express itself unchecked in this one small corner of the Swiss Alps. The sensitive and observant visitor who accepts these limitations will not go unrewarded in the valleys of the Park.

There are a number of valleys, mostly forested naturally and quite densely, that are contained within the National Park's area of almost 17,000 hectares (169 square kilometres). Most, but not all of them, have official paths wandering through and over high passes, thus enabling short walks and lengthy tours to be undertaken. Routes outlined below represent a selection of the area's main features, and on them there are good opportunities to observe marmots or deer, chamois or ibex in their natural surroundings. But while the sighting of various animals will no doubt be something of a boost to the walker's day, it is the sense of wilderness, of an untracked country-side, that is the essence of this National Park. The paths we wander will mostly be clear and well-defined, yet the countryside all around has an untamed character that is unchallenged anywhere else in Switzerland.

It was in 1906 that the idea for a National Park in Switzerland was first mooted. But it was no easy thing to find a suitable location, for in a small country such as this, with high mountains, extensive glaciers and lakes and permanent snowfields, and with essential industries reducing accessible agricultural land to a minimum, there were few enough corners left in their natural state that would conform to the demanding standards set by the initiators of the scheme. However, in the Lower Engadine was found such an area that had escaped much of the industrial or commercial exploitation of a large proportion of Switzerland, and in 1909 an agreement was drawn up with the community of Zernez for the leasing of twenty square kilometres of Val Cluozza. It was seen then that the Lower Engadine's adjacent valleys were sparsely populated. There were large areas of natural forest and high meadow that had been but little used, and by resettling a few farmers in the Engadine proper, it would be possible to enlarge the Park's boundaries in the ensuing years.

On August 1st 1914 the National Park was officially founded, and since that date the various communes of Zernez, S-chanf, Scuol and Valchava have all contributed land to enable the *Schweizerische Bund Für Naturschutz* (Swiss Society for the Protection of Nature) to enlarge the Park to its present size.

As a natural reserve protected from human interference, even the grazing of domestic cattle, goats or sheep have been forbidden. No trees have been felled, no planting or hunting, and Nature has been left to evolve virtually unhindered. Flowers are there in abundance, especially in June and early July; but it is the possibility of catching sight of wildlife that keeps the walker alert. There are ibex at the head of Val Trupchun, marmots at Alp Grimmels and elsewhere, chamois on many slopes and deer throughout the forests. When the Park was first set up there were no red deer in Switzerland, but large herds began to migrate from the Austrian Tyrol, and today there may be as many as two thousand roaming through the Park during the summer. In the autumn each year, these herds drift away again to winter else-where.

Although camping and bivouacking are both banned from the Park itself, there are campsites beyond its borders at Cinuos-chel, Zernez and Scuol. The only overnight lodgings to be had within the Park are at Blockhaus Cluozza, a lovely old rustic inn tucked among larches high above the Ova da Cluozza at the end of a three-hour walk from Zernez, or at Hotel Il Fuorn on the Ofen Pass road. Both are extremely busy in the main season and will need to be booked in advance. Just outside the boundaries, the Varüsh Hut is situated in charming countryside in the lower reaches of Val Trupchun. It offers *matratzenlager* accommodation and a simple meals service.

Before departing on any of the walks described below, a visit to the National Park House at Zernez is highly recommended. This is found on the outskirts of the town a short distance from the main centre, along the Ofen Pass road. There you will be able to browse among the many fascinating exhibits, collect an armful of informative leaflets (but little in English), guidebooks, picture books and maps; or attend one of the film shows given during summer evenings.

In conclusion, the following regulations are outlined for your information. Do not be put off by them; they have been carefully drawn up in the very best interests of a unique area. Most ramblers, I am sure, will not find themselves unnecessarily restricted. If you wish to roam at will across hillsides away from marked paths, there will be plenty of opportunities to do so in other parts of the Engadine. If you enjoy an overnight bivouac, look beyond the Park. Wander the paths here with your eyes and ears tuned, for there is so much to absorb.

Extracts from the National Park Regulations:
1. Children under 15 years of age may enter the Park only when accompanied by adults: school parties and youth groups between 15 and 20 years only when in the charge of a responsible leader.
2. Parties of more than twenty visitors and schools must apply beforehand to the Park authorities.
3. Shooting and fishing within the areas of the Park are strictly forbidden.

   Futhermore it is forbidden:
   to light fires, camp out, leave litter;
   to kill or injure animals, to catch or trap them, or to disturb them in any way;
   to remove or damage nesting-places, eggs or young birds;
   to dig up, tear up or damage plants (including mushrooms);
   to pick flowers, gather berries, to cut or collect wood;
   to graze cattle;
   to introduce firearms, traps, specimen boxes or botanical presses into the Park;
   to take dogs into the area, even when on a leash;
   to take moving pictures for commercial purposes.

Route 74: S-chanf (1,669m) - Varüsch Hut (1,736m)

Grade: 1
Distance: 3 kilometres
Height gain: 67 metres
Time: 1 hour

From the Engadine proper there are two or three short walking routes to the Varüsch hut, and it is also possible to drive to the entrance of Val Trupchun where there is a car park, and to walk from there. The valley itself is most pleasant, with green meadows and forest, and soft views in all directions.

A sign near the church in S-chanf indicates the route to take. A village street leads down to the river, crosses it and the new bypass road beyond, and cuts across the valley meadows as a broad track. Follow this for a short distance, then branch off to the right on a trail leading towards the forest. This soon swings left and contours round into the shaft of Val Trupchun. Ignore alternative paths leading off to the right, but as you come to a side valley (Val da Scrigns) bear left and drop down to the confluence of streams; Ova da Varüsch in the main valley, and Ova da Chaschauna coming from the little valley to the right. Cross over onto the north bank of Ova da Varüsch, turn right and wander along a broad track, shortly to reach the Varüsch hut, idyllically set in meadows, with a restaurant adjacent. *(Matratzen-lager* accommodation for 25. Open from June to October.)

Alternatively, follow the road leading into the valley from the car park, continue along the track without difficulty all the way to the hut.

Route 75: Varüsch Hut (1,736m) - Alp Trupchun (2,040m)

Grade: 2
Distance: 4 kilometres
Height gain: 304 metres
Time: 1½ hours

In the early stages of summer the pastures of Alp Trupchun are heavily grazed by deer, chamois and even ibex, although ibex tend to remain as high as possible. In the cool of morning, or in the evening, it is possible to see large herds of red deer on this walk. Later, as summer develops, it may well be necessary to extend this walk beyond Alp Trupchun as far as the pass at the head of the valley, Fuorcla Trupchun (2,782m), in order to catch sight of wildlife, but in any case, it is always delightful to wander through the meadowlands with their flowers, whether or not there are animals to see.

From the hut take the trail leading up-valley along the bank of the stream. There are lovely views. After about ten minutes or so, the way enters the National Park, announced by a large informative notice board. Continue along the northern bank of the stream, but after a while the path is led across to its south side and comes to a junction of paths by the old building of Alp Purchér. Continue ahead in the same direction, then cross back to the north side of the stream after about 200 metres, to the entrance of Val Müschauns. Here there is another path junction. Take the right fork still heading up-valley, leaving the left-hand path to enter the Müschauns glen on its way to Fuorcla Val Sassa. (See Route 76)

The Trupchun trail gradually rises up the valley, following the stream all the way, and reaches Alp Trupchun without diverting from its course.

For an extension to Fuorcla Trupchun, continue up-valley on the north side of the stream, to climb steeply towards the pass. As an alternative return to the Varüsch hut, go down beyond Alp Trupchun, then cross to the south side of the stream on a path that climbs the hillside in forest shade. It wanders down-valley some way above the stream as far as Val Scrigns coming in from the left. Turn right here and drop down to the main stream and cross it on a junction of paths. Now bear right to reach the hut.

Route 76: Varüsch Hut (1,736m) - Blockhaus Cluozza (1,880m)

Grade: 2-3
Distance: 13 kilometres
Height gain: 1,121 metres   Height loss: 1,025 metres
Time: 6½ hours

This walk is one of the recommended stages on a traverse of the National Park. (See Route 84) It's not always a clear trail, especially should the clouds hang low, but under normal summer conditions there will be no real difficulty for the reasonably experienced mountain trekker. The route contrasts between soft valley meadowlands and loose screes and snow patches. It climbs steeply to cross the pass of Fuorcla Val Sassa (2,857m) on the southern shoulder of Piz Quattervals, highest peak in the National Park, and drops into the tight wedge of Val Cluozza where the silver stream leaps through its bed of rocks, before rising up to find the hut set amid the trees.

Blockhaus Cluozza, National Park

Blockhaus Cluozza is owned by the National Park authorities. It can accommodate 70 in bedrooms and *matratzenlager* dormitories, and has a thriving restaurant service with meals and drinks available to casual visitors as well as for overnight guests. Because of high-season popularity, it will most likely be necessary to book accommodation in advance. This can be done through the local tourist office in Zernez. (Address: Verkehrsverein, CH 7530 Zernez. Tel:082/8 13 00)

Follow Route 75 directions from the Varüsch hut to the junction of paths at the entrance to Val Müschauns. Take the left fork on a path that crosses the Ova da Müschauns on a wooden bridge, then turn right to head up-valley. The route, faint at times, is marked with paint flashes; it leads among sparse woods and patches of gentians, with Piz Quattervals rearing overhead. Then the path recrosses the stream to its eastern bank (true left bank) and rises above the stream among dwarf pines. Working round to the east it climbs more steeply, goes over a stream and heads up to a grassy bluff. Between the bluff and the pass there is a gaunt basin to traverse, then the way zig-zags up to screes, with a small tarn seen off to the right. Shortly after you come onto Fuorcla Val Sassa with its interesting views that include not only the immediate Park area, with its dark forests trapped in steep valley wedges, but also southward to the snow peaks of the Bernina and its neighbours on the skyline.

The descent on the east side of the pass runs north-eastwards over scree and snow slopes into the glacial basin of Val Sassa. As with part of the ascent, this section could be difficult in poor visibility, but there are paint flashes to guide you. Below the snow patches cairns aid the route, although normally there will be no difficulty in locating the correct line to follow. On reaching the stream wander down its left bank and eventually reach the junction with Val dal Diavel entering from the right. Bear left and continue on the left bank heading downstream. On being joined by the path coming down from Valletta on your left, cross the stream on a bridge and follow the path uphill above the right bank. Soon after there is another path junction. Take the left fork, and a few moments later you will come to Blockhaus Cluozza.

Route 77:   Zernez (1,472m) - Blockhaus Cluozza (1,880m)

Grade: 2
Distance: 6 kilometres
Height gain: 650 metres   Height loss: 320 metres
Time: 3 hours

Val Cluozza is densely forested. As you climb steeply up the hillside an hour or so from Zernez, there is a brief 'window' in the trees and a sudden panorama is revealed to show the deep cut of valley stretching off to the south; a seemingly impenetrable blanket of pine and larch covering its lower to middle reaches, and bare mountains rising from it with scratch marks of streams carved in their sides. It's a view that displays better than most the great scenic differences between valleys of the National Park and those of the Bregaglia, for example - another world away. This could almost be Canada.

The walk to Blockhaus Cluozza is along a steep switchback of a trail. The path is well-trodden, but it zig-zags tightly among the forests to gain access to Val Cluozza over a shoulder of mountain before levelling out for a short traverse of the hillsides. Then it drops to the valley floor, crosses the stream and climbs steeply up to the hut, set as it is on a clifftop amid larch and pine trees from where red deer may be seen feeding in early mornings and evening time.

The hut is at the junction of several routes. It serves as a halfway house for those making a traverse of the Park. It serves as a base for

Val Cluozza, in the National Park

others studying the wildlife of the region, for those enjoying leisurely walks in this unique corner; or as a lunch-stop for a round-trip from Zernez.

The path begins about one kilometre beyond the National Park House in Zernez, on the road leading to the Ofen Pass. On the right-hand side of the road there is a covered wooden bridge and a National Park notice board. Car parking nearby. Cross the bridge and follow a farm track through terraced meadowland towards the forest. The track enters the forest and begins to gain height in long sweeps, soon to become a path of beaten earth that zig-zags steeply up the rounded spur of mountain which forms the western gateway to Val Cluozza. It's a fragrant walk among the pines, with red squirrels in the branches overhead, and prospects of seeing deer through the trees. An hour after leaving the road the path enters the National Park, although for some time it has followed along its edge. Now and then there is a brief glimpse of the valley stretching ahead in the south, but at last the path tops a bluff (2,122m) and there are lovely vistas of forest, valley and mountain to be had.

The way continues along the hillside way above the valley. A narrow path, in places it crosses minor streams flowing down, or bare-earth scars where spring avalanches have swept through the trees. Then it drops steeply to the valley, passes what once must have been an alp, then crosses the Ova da Cluozza on a wooden bridge to climb the final slopes on the eastern side of the stream, so to reach the blockhaus.

Route 78: Blockhaus Cluozza (1,880m) - Murtér (2,545m) - Hotel Il Fuorn (1,794m)

Grade: 2
Distance: 12 kilometres
Height gain: 665 metres   Height loss: 751 metres
Time: 6½ hours

Another stage on the traverse of the National Park, this day's walk climbs over a high grassy sadle and descends through forest to the Ofen Pass road. There may well be sightings of marmots in the one-time alpine meadows, while from the Murtér ridge you might possibly spy chamois grazing.

From the blockhaus take the path leading up-valley (reversing the approach route from Varüsch) to the junction of paths. Take the left-hand trail heading uphill through forest. When you emerge from the trees there are flower-bright pastures to cross, and then climbing steeply in zig-zags towards the pass. This is reached in about two hours from Blockhaus Cluozza; a good place to rest for a while to enjoy the views and to scan the hillsides and ridges for sight of chamois.

On the eastern side of the Murtér saddle, the path loses height through more meadowlands walling the Val dal Spöl, and eventually enters larch forests towards the foot of the slope. The path swings right and reaches a junction of trails and a large sign. A short stroll left here will lead to the road; but our route forks right, climbing for a moment, then levelling to a traverse of the hillside above the river. For a little over three kilometres the path wanders through the woods above the river, climbing and falling and twisting round spurs of mountain, until at last it slopes down to cross the Spöl by way of Punt Periv, a sturdy bridge. Now bearing left, the track heads up to a crossing of God la Schera. A track joins from the right and the way continues up to the forested saddle (1,833m) beyond which the trail slopes off to the Ofen Pass road. (There is an alternative path branching off to the right just after the saddle; this swings in long loops to the east, then heads north round the edge of Munt la Schera to gain the road at a point some way higher than the main track.) Whichever route is adopted, once the road is reached turn right and walk along it to Hotel Il Fuorn.

Despite the proximity of the road, the meadows near the hotel are often grazed by herds of red deer during the evening and early morning. The hotel is rather more up-market than other establishments mentioned in this guide, but there is *matratzenlager* accommodation to be had across the road from the hotel with meals available in a hotel dining room set aside for the specific use of *matratzenlager* guests.

**Route 79:   Il Fuorn (1,794m) - Stabelchod (1,958m) -
           Margunet (2,308m) - Il Fuorn**

Grade: 2
Distance: 8.5 kilometres
Height gain: 514 metres   Height loss: 514 metres
Time: 3 hours

This walk follows the National Park Nature Trail *(Naturlehrpfad)*, and along it will be found various information points explaining the particular sites of interest. For anyone wishing for more information than can be obtained from the explanation boards, there are various publications available at the National Park House in Zernez. Of particular interest is the five-language guide to the Nature Trail, and for the more studious, a comprehensive scientific study of the whole Park entitled; *Through the Swiss National Park* which was published in 1966 and printed with an English language edition. It is an invaluable guide to the geology of the area, as well as to the flora and fauna found there.

The walk itself is an interesting one which follows a forest track for part of the way, crosses streams and meadows, climbs fairly steeply through one stream-cut valley to another, and gives ample opportunities to see chamois and red deer along the way.

Leaving Il Fuorn (Postbus from Zernez, or car parking beside the road at parking place No.6, for those with their own transport), cross to the south side of the river and follow it upstream where you will find a number of explanatory boards along the way. The path crosses a side stream flowing in from Val Chavagl through forest on the right, and shortly after crosses the main Ova dal Fuorn to its north bank. One path heads up to the road here, but for our walk stay beside the river and take the forest track leading between the river and the road for about 15 minutes. As you come to another side stream (this one flowing from the left) bear left and cross the road at parking area No.9. The path ahead leads into Val Stabelchod, and on reaching the former alp of Stabelchod there will be seen another trail dropping away to the left. This leads back to the road. Ignore this and continue ahead through forest cover again, climbing steadily. There are more explanatory boards along the trail.

The path becomes a little more steep, veering away from the stream and zig-zagging up to the saddle of Margunet which effectively divides the valleys of Stabelchod and dal Botsch. From this point you can often see red deer and chamois, and fine views are to be had over the valley. To continue, descend by way of Val dal Botsch, keeping alert for the chance of seeing more animals. At the head of the valley Fuorcla dal Botsch allows access to Val Plavna and the lovely Val Mingèr. Our path joins the track by the stream, but ignores the temptation of going higher and instead continues down-valley towards forest once more. The trail emerges from the dense forest at parking area No.7. Cross the road and retrace the path through the forest, over the Fuorn stream and back to Il Fuorn.

Route 80: Il Fuorn (Parking Area No.2) (1,808m) -
Alp Grimmels (2,055m) - Ova Spin (1,838m)

Grade: 1-2
Distance: 5.5 kilometres
Height gain: 247 metres   Height loss: 217 metres
Time: 2-2½ hours

Walking this path one bright June day with my family, I saw many red deer and chamois grazing along the edge of the forest, and sat watching marmots at close range for maybe an hour while we picnicked in the designated shelter at Alp Grimmels. In the woods there were patches of snow left from winter, but out in the open it had mostly gone, to be replaced by banks of flowers; soldanellas and alpine anemones, and acres of crocus.

The first part of the walk climbs steeply away from the road, but having gained height it eases and thereafter becomes a gentle stroll with fine views and always plenty of interest.

From parking area No.2 between Zernez and Il Fuorn, cross the road and take the footpath leading into forest on the eastern side. The path soon comes to a junction, but ignore the right-hand trail and continue on, climbing up through patchy forest which eventually leads to an opening with the cropped meadowland of Alp Grimmels ahead. As you approach it there are views spreading off to the right along the valley to the Ofen Pass, and ahead into the Val Ftur, which looks extremely attractive, but alas there is no authorised path into it.

At Alp Grimmels there is a small wooden shelter, a designated resting place. From it ramblers can often watch marmots at play, or see deer or chamois grazing nearby. The views are lovely, and there will inevitably be flowers to pattern the sloping meadows all around. Sit quietly and keep your eyes alert for the sign of wildlife.

The path continues across the alp and comes to another trail junction; the path which heads off right slopes down to reach Il Fuorn, but ours goes straight ahead through a broad gully and over the somewhat boggy saddle of Champlönch where more deer may well be seen. Now following a stream the path gradually slopes down to the road once more at the parking area of Ova Spin (No.1). From here Postbuses run down-valley to Zernez and up-valley to Il Fuorn. If you left a car at parking area No.2, simply turn left and wander up the road for another kilometre or so.

144

Route 81: **Buffalora (1,968m) - Munt la Schera (2,586m) -**
Il Fuorn (1,794m)

Grade: 2
Distance: 11 kilometres
Height gain: 618 metres   Height loss: 792 metres
Time: 5 hours

The *Wegerhaus Buffalora* is situated on the National Park boundary
just short of the Ofen Pass uphill from Il Fuorn. (Accommodation
available; Postbus stop; car parking.) From it a number of paths head
off, not only into the Park, but also through neighbouring valleys and
over passes that lead to distant villages. This walk is not too-demand-
ing, and it gives fine views, opportunities to catch sight of red deer,
and an interesting day's outing.

Leave the road and cross the Fuorn stream on a clear path leading
steadily uphill southward to reach Alp Buffalora (2,038m). You may
well see edelweiss growing here. The path continues, climbing now in
forest, veering a little to the left before swinging back to an upper alp,
Marangun (2,194m) some way below the crags of Munt Buffalora.
This area is also sometimes known as Alp Buffalora, and from it there
leads an interesting walk south, through Jufplaun to the back-country
of Val Mora. Our walk, however, heads westward (the right fork)
from the alp huts, wandering along the hillside gaining height to enter
the National Park through a little saddle between Munt Chavagl and
point 2,437m.

Ahead rises the dome of Munt la Schera. The path bears half-left to
traverse round the south side of the hill, but there is a right fork in the
path giving the opportunity to wander to the summit, which is gained
in about 2¾ hours from Buffalora. Views from here are delightful.
Looking south you gaze over forest slopes, beyond the Park's
boundary and down into the Italian Val del Gallo to the extensive lake
that leads into Livigno. Eastwards there's the hint of Val Müstair,
green, warm, lush. Northward other mountains lead into the Lower
Engadine, while out to the west forest and mountain take the eye
towards the flood plain in which Zernez sits.

Drop down from the summit of Munt la Schera to regain the main
traversing path. Bear right and follow it to Alp la Schera (2,091m)
where the trail divides. Take the right fork and follow this path back
to the road, which you reach a short distance west of Il Fuorn.

Route 82: **Il Fuorn (1,794m) - Fuorcla Val Dal Botsch (2,678m) -**
Il Foss (2,317m) - Val S-charl (1,664m)

Grade: 3
Distance: 13 kilometres
Height gain: 884 metres   Height loss   1,014m
Time: 6¾ hours

A fairly strenuous day's walking, this effectively completes a traverse
of the National Park if taken from S-chanf in the Upper Engadine.
(See Route 84 for the full itinerary.) On this stretch there are two
passes to cross, but there will fortunately not be too much height to
lose and then regain between them. Below Il Foss the route descends
into the superb Val Mingèr with its forests of arolla pine. This in turn
leads to the Val S-charl. From here it is a long (12 kilometres) walk
down-valley to Scuol in the Lower Engadine, but the little village of
S-charl lies only three kilometres up-valley, and *pension* accommodation can be had there. Alternatively, you may be lucky enough to
catch a Postbus down to the Engadine.

From Il Fuorn take the path leading up-valley on the south side of
Ova dal Fuorn as far as the first path junction. Go left here, cross the
road and enter Val dal Botsch. The route through this valley goes first
through forest, only slightly gaining height until the stream is reached.
It then follows the stream with views ahead looking up to the pass.
Along this rising valley there will be prospects of seeing chamois. The
way divides after some time; take the left fork, straight ahead on a zig-
zag climb up grass slopes, and shortly before reaching the pass (about
2½ hours from Il Fuorn) the grass is traded for rocks.

Fuorcla Val dal Botsch has a fine panorama. Way off to the south
you can just see the Bernina peaks over a jumble of intermediary
ridges. To the north rise the so-called Engadine Dolomites. It's all
lovely country. Il Foss, the next pass to tackle, lies a little east of
north, across a glacial cirque that forms the head of Val Plavna. To
reach it requires a steep descent to a couple of streams in the bowl of
the cirque, followed by a short pull up to the pass. (About 1½ hours
from Fuorcla Val dal Botsch to Il Foss.)

This pass is green and pleasant, and with a wonderful view of Piz
Plavna Dadaint (3,166m) immediately behind to the west; a fine peak
with fingers of rock piercing from its south ridge. Now ahead comes a
descent of great charm, through meadows and forest down into Val
Mingèr. It's a delight all the way, with streams and soft turf under
foot, and views into the S-charl valley below. On reaching this main
valley you pass out of the National Park. Reach the unmade road at

Mingèrbrücke flood control, where there is a Postbus pick-up point. For the Lower Engadine (Scuol) head left. For S-charl village, turn right.

Route 83: S-charl (Mingèrbrücke) (1,664m) - Val Mingèr - Il Foss (2,317m)

Grade: 1-2
Distance: 8 kilometres
Height gain: 653 metres
Time: 3 hours

Val Mingèr is a delightful glen of flower meadows, forests of cembra and arolla pine and dashing streams with superb views of the dolomitic peak of Piz Plavna Dadaint (3,166m) peering over the pass of Il Foss at the head of the valley to the west. A day's wandering through this valley will be a day well spent, whether or not you decide go to as far as the pass. Chamois are often to be seen on the slopes of Piz Mingèr, while red deer are in the forests and, at certain times of the day, may also be seen grazing in the open meadows.

Either drive or take the Postbus from S-charl (or Scuol) to the flood control at Mingèrbrücke about 3.5 kilometres north-west of S-charl village. A footpath sign here directs you to the start of the walk on the far side of the stream. At once the path plunges into forest and begins to gain height easily as it enters the Val Mingèr. Before long the path leads out of the trees and across a small close-cropped meadow with pleasant views ahead. Across this you are back among trees again, but soon the valley divides, and between the two branches there stands a curious sandstone outcrop off to the left, known as the 'Witch's Head'. This has been carved by water, wind and frost over countless centuries into assorted interesting shapes, among them the face of a witch and a raven's head. An information board beside the path gives an explanation of the geological history that has resulted in the formations seen.

There is only one path leading through the valley, and that heads up the right-hand branch, in and out of forest, across meadowlands, crossing and recrossing the stream; always with lovely views ahead. On reaching the log hut of Mingèr Dadaint (2,090m), Piz Plavna Dadaint seems to grow in stature over the green saddle of Il Foss above. From this point look out for sign of chamois, deer and marmots.

Beyond Mingèr Dadaint the path swings left, then arcs westward to

147

gain the pass. The views from here are splendid in all directions.

Route 84: A Traverse of the National Park

Grade: 3
Distance: 41 kilometres
Height gain: (accumulative):   2,737 metres
Height loss: (accumulative):   2,790 metres
Time: 3-4 days

By combining several of the routes previously described, it is possible to undertake a traverse of the National Park from south-west to north-east, thereby gaining satisfaction, not only from the pleasures of a multi-day tour, but also from seeing a broad spectrum of the Park's scenery and the very real chance of watching plenty of wildlife along the way. It is an interesting tour, and one that would make very good use of four days' holiday. To ensure accommodation at the end of each day's stage, it is advisable to check first on the availability of space -especially during the mid-season months of July and August. Enquiries should be addressed either to the National Park House in Zernez, or to Zernez Informational Office. Remember, camping is strictly forbidden within the National Park's boundaries.

Begin the walk at S-chanf in the Upper Engadine and wander into Val Trupchun (Route 74) as far as the Varüsch hut. Beyond the hut the way goes deeper into the valley before turning off into Val Müschauns and climbing over Fuorcla Val Sassa (Route 76) and dropping down to the bed of Val Cluozza in order to reach Blockhaus Cluozza for an overnight lodging. There then follows a steep climb to the ridge of Murtèr with its extensive views and opportunities to see chamois. Beyond Murtèr the route descends to the valley road at Il Fuorn (Route 78).

Having completed the crossing of the southern section of the Park, there follows a long day's journey over the two passes of Fuorcla Val dal Botsch and Il Foss (Route 82), then wandering down through Val Mingèr to the S-charl valley and the completion of the traverse.

Overnight accommodation in the Varüsch hut, Blockhaus Cluozza, Il Fuorn and S-charl.

LOWER ENGADINE - NORTH-EASTERN REGION (ZERNEZ TO MARTINA)

Position:	North-eastwards from the junction of the main Engadine road and that of the Ofen Pass at Zernez, to the point where the River Inn flows into Austria below Martina.
Maps:	Landeskarte der Schweiz 1:50,000 series Nos.249 'Tarasp' and 259 'Ofenpass' 1:100,000 series No.39 'Flüelapass'
Valley Bases:	Zernez (1,472m), Scuol (1,430m)
Huts:	Linard Hut (2,327m), Tuoi Hut (2,250m), Lischana Hut (2,500m)

Whilst the hillsides that form a natural terrace along the north wall of the valley offer some extremely pleasant walking, the main attractions here will be found in exploring those minor valleys that cut deep into the mountains on either side. Each one has its own distinctive atmosphere. Each one has something rather special about it, and a holiday based in this corner will have much to commend it.

In the bed of the valley, the Inn river foams and swirls through gorges and low meadows; a great challenge to white-water canoe enthusiasts. It is a serious stretch of river that should only be tackled by experts. The meadows that line it are mostly caught between river and forest. Here and there are hay barns, but halfway along the valley it broadens out to allow communities like Tarasp, Fontana and Vulpera to exploit their sunny positions. The valley floor is undulating here, and Tarasp Castle occupies a steep hilltop plug overlooking lush pastures, a small tarn, and the very attractive village to which it gives its name. From every corner of the village there is a view that screams out to be photographed; a calendar photographer's dream.

The majority of Lower Engadine villages, however, are found on the north bank of the Inn; some in the valley bottom where the land allows, but others planted with care upon the hillside shelves above the valley, catching the sun, enjoying lovely views.

Of the minor valleys projecting into the high Silvretta mountains to the north, perhaps the best is Val Tuoi, but Val Tasna and Val Sinestra also have their undisputed charms, as does the narrow, steep-walled Val Lavinuoz. On the southern side Val S-charl is a long, secretive valley that suddenly opens out to a wonderland of streams, side valleys, meadows and mountains. Running along its edge is the north-eastern boundary of the National Park. At its head are easy passes leading out to Val Müstair.

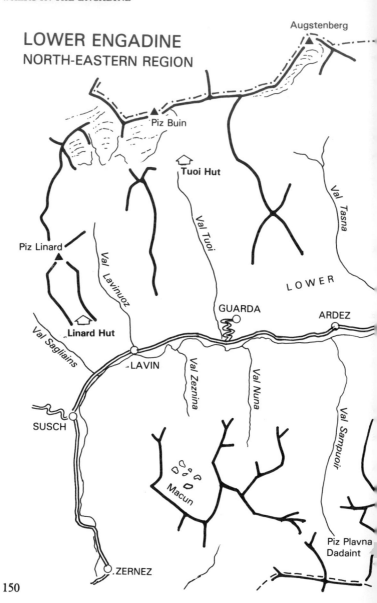

LOWER ENGADINE
NORTH-EASTERN REGION

Augstenberg

Piz Buin

Tuoi Hut

Val Tasna

Piz Linard

Val Lavinuoz

Val Tuoi

GUARDA

LOWER

ARDEZ

Linard Hut

Val Sagliains

LAVIN

Val Zeznina

Val Nuna

Val Sampuoir

SUSCH

Macun

Piz Plavna
Dadaint

ZERNEZ

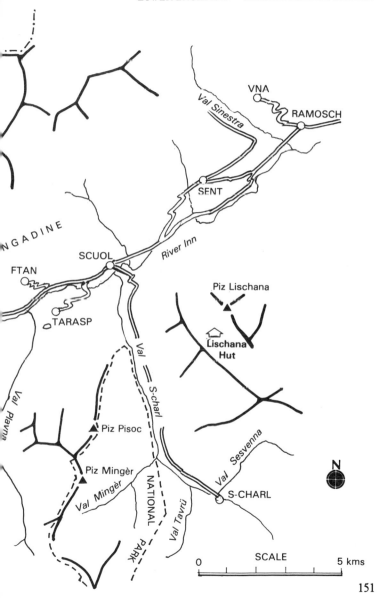

West of Val S-charl there's Val Plavna that offers an enticing long trek with options at its head. In this valley are some fabulous dolomitic peaks to catch the attention and retain it. Next comes Val Sampuoir, then very steep little hanging valleys that lead up into the mountains blocking Zernez, and affording views north to the snows of the higher Silvretta peaks that form the border with Austria opposite.

Whilst offering an entirely different type of scenery to that of the Upper Engadine, or indeed, of the Bregaglia, the Lower Engadine is by no means a poor substitute. No walker or general mountain lover need ever go away disappointed.

Route 85:   Zernez (1,472m) - Carolina (1,568m) -
Cinuos-Chel (1,613m)

Grade: 1
Distance: 9.5 kilometres
Height gain: 141 metres
Time: 2½ hours

A gentle valley stroll across meadowlands and through forests along the edge of the National Park, this is an undemanding yet very pleasant morning or afternoon's outing. It could be extended as far as S-chanf or Zuoz, or indeed as part of a long-distance Engadine traverse. On the other hand, it could be used as an approach to the Varüsch hut in Val Trupchun, while as a walk on its own it is a most satisfactory way of spending two and a half hours.

There are two choices by which to begin this walk. The first is to walk south of Zernez on the up-valley road to a point where the road makes a sharp right-hand bend. On the left a footpath breaks away, crosses the railway line and comes to a junction of paths. Turn right here on the trail to Carolina.

The alternative start is from the Zernez to Ofen Pass road, about one kilometre beyond the National Park House. There is a covered wooden bridge on the right-hand side of the road, and a large National Park notice board. (See start of Route 77.) Cross the bridge, and where the track forks, take the right branch to wander through the broad flat meadows to follow parallel with the railway. At cross-paths join the other choice of trail (above) from Zernez, and walk straight ahead.

Through pine and larch woods the path wanders steadily towards the little area of Carolina - an isolated station on the railway. Here and there other paths branch away, or cross ours. Mostly these are heading up to the National Park boundary, but the course of our route continues to monitor the line of the railway and river, until at last the three come together with Cinuos-chel seen on the opposite bank. Cross over by way of the bridge and go up to the village. Return to Zernez by either train or Postbus.

Route 86:   Zernez (1,472m) - Lavin (1,412m)

Grade: 1
Distance: 9.5 kilometres
Height loss: 60 metres
Time: 2-2½ hours

Another low valley walk, this follows the River Inn as it flows northwards through the narrow cut it has made in the mountains just beyond Zernez. As with Route 85 above, this walk could conveniently be extended much farther along the valley, for there are continuing paths that go to Ardez, to Fontana or Tarasp or Scuol, or beyond even to Sur En and far beyond this and over the frontier to reach the little town of Nauders in Austria. A valley walk it is, to catch the flavour of forest and meadow, the River Inn surging along to one side, the mountains rising steeply on the other. As you round the bend just after Susch the valley opens out and spreads itself more towards the east in a long hint of brightness, as a soft light floods down the hillsides.

In Zernez, where the road from the Ofen Pass joins the main Engadine highway, a church with a tall and elegant spire stands back a little from the road junction. A footpath goes round to the left of it. This is the path to take. It leads along the foot of the hill slope with the river snaking in wide loops off to the left. Where the path forks, bear right to gain height away from the river towards a wooded knoll with an open patch of pasture and farm buildings in it. This is Muotta dal Clüs (1,685m)

Beyond Clüs the path slopes down to the level of the river bank, passing more farm buildings, but another sidles away to the right to traverse the hillside at a steady angle, coming down again to meet the low path a little to the east of Susch. Either path will be acceptable. For much of the way so far the lofty cone of Piz Linard has dominated the valley, but on rounding the curve of the Inn, other views open out. Stay with the lower path now and make for a bridge over the river that leads up to the little village of Lavin. From here Postbuses and trains link with Zernez.

Route 87: Zernez (1,472m) - Alp Laschadura (1,998m) -
Fuorcla Stragliavita (2,687m) - Alp Sampuoir (1,854m) -
Ardez Station (1,432m)

Grade: 3
Distance: 16 kilometres
Height gain: 1,215 metres   Height loss: 1,255 metres
Time: 7½ hours

Zernez nestles below the western point of a large triangle wedge of
mountains formed by the valleys of the Lower Engadine, the Spöl-Val
Müstair (bridged by the Ofen Pass) and the Italian Adige. This route
cuts across that wedge at almost its narrowest point. Even so, it is a
crossing that is fairly strenuous, but interesting all the way, with
opportunities for some fine views and a rich collection of alpine
flowers on both sides of the pass.

Head away from Zernez on the Ofen Pass road for about three kilometres. At various points along the road there are paths leading off
that will head into the Val Laschadura, the first real valley cutting
away to the left as you head up this road. Perhaps the most obvious
starting point comes about an hour from Zernez at a sharp hairpin
bend with the valley slanting away from it. A path leads directly into
the valley to reach the substantial buildings of Alp Laschadura after
another kilometre. The path, marked with red and white paint
flashes, continues deeper into the valley, following along the left-hand
side of the stream until, having reached a little building (Margun;
2,210m), it begins to climb in earnest up the north slope.

Fuorcla Stragliavita is the saddle formed by the linking ridges of Piz
Nun and Ils Cuogns, and from it there are shafted views over the
National Park region to the south where Val Cluozza is so heavily
forested, and down to the valleys flowing into the Lower Engadine to
the north. Above the Engadine rise peaks of the Silvretta group, their
snowfields and small glaciers gleaming under the sun.

The pass is reached in about four hours from Zernez; a sharp ascent,
but there is a longish descent ahead. (There is a signpost on the
saddle.) The way goes down into the rough bowl of rock and scree,
with snow patches until mid-summer, heading north-eastwards
following paint flashes on a gentle slope that steepens towards the little
hut of Plan Surröven (2,256m). From here the way becomes clearer as
you drop into the bed of the valley of Sampuoir among alpenroses and
a lush tangled vegetation. Alp Sampuoir lies an hour and a half below
the pass. Beyond it stretches forest, with fine mountains on the far
side of the Engadine. Above on either side the mountains rise steeply,

here squeezing the valley, but opening with promise ahead. The way follows down beside the stream, becomes a track that loops off to meet the Inn, then up a road to Ardez station.

Route 88: Lavin (1,412m) - Linard Hut (2,327m)

Grade:	3
Distance:	4.5 kilometres
Height gain:	915 metres
Time:	2½ hours

Piz Linard is a high conical peak that overlooks the Engadine from its prominent position above the valley's north-east curve between Susch and Lavin. It imposes itself upon those who wander in and around Zernez by dominating the skyline, although it has little significance to those villages along the main shaft of the valley, to whom it is just another part of the long north wall of the Lower Engadine. The south-west and south-east ridges of Piz Linard plunge steeply down to contain within their embrace the little Val Glims. And it is in this valley, with the broken face of the mountain rearing behind, that the Linard hut is to be found.

Unlike several other mountain huts owned by the SAC mentioned in this guide, the Linard hut is a modest shelter with room for 43 people. It has a guardian from the middle of June until the end of October, but meals are not provided.

The path from Lavin ducks beneath the railway to the left of the stream flowing from Val Lavinuoz, and climbs the hillside west of the village aiming towards the forest slopes. It is a broad track, clear and obvious, and it swings in long loops up through the forest to reach an isolated alp hut set in a clearing at 1,957 metres. The path from here is less broad, and it slants away towards the left, coming above the forest and over grassy slopes, with fine views back into the Engadine with tiny villages far below, and the river snaking off towards Zernez. The path continues now to make an easy-angled traverse below the south-east ridge of Piz Linard, then zig-zags up to gain the hut.

From the hut there is a foreshortened view of Piz Linard, but it still appears rather formidable, although there are some moderately demanding routes on it. For added interest, energy and time willing, continue past the hut and enter the tight cirque towards the head of Val Glims. Aim towards the centre of the valley to find a couple of little tarns, or from these bear left and go up the slopes to the obvious pass of Fuorcla da Glims (2,802m) about 1½ hours from the hut.

There you will have a marvellous panorama of folding ridges across the depths of Val Sagliains. Across this valley, looking a little north-west, there is seen the Vereinapass (reached in another hour and a half) which gives access to a long valley leading out towards Klosters.

An alternative, but much longer, return to Lavin other than a reversal of the approach walk, entails crossing Fuorcla da Glims into the head of Val Sagliains, then descending this all the way down to its opening between Lavin and Susch. A fine circuit of about 6½ hours; Lavin to Lavin.

Route 89: Lavin (1,412m) - Alp Zeznina Dadaint (1,958m) - Macun Tarns (2,616m)

Grade: 2-3
Distance: 8 kilometres
Height gain: 1,204 metres
Time: 4 hours

On the south side of the Lower Engadine, opposite Lavin, the mountains are carved into horseshoe cirques; Macun (Zeznina), Nuna and Sampuoir. High in the Macun cirque lie dotted a number of little tarns. This outing makes a point of visiting them. There is a lot of height to gain, and in so doing there are various vegetation zones to pass through. Two alps are visited; Zeznina Dadoura and Zeznina Dadaint. Forests lead to these, but beyond them are grass slopes becoming rough and wild above, where screes and jumbled rocks take over.

Cross the Inn below Lavin and bear left on a track beside the river. But shortly after fork right on the continuing track heading alongside the forest. After crossing the stream issuing from Val Zeznina, the way begins to climb in loops up the forested hillside to reach the clearing of Zeznina Dadoura (1,817m) with its hut, after about two hours from Lavin. Having gained more than four hundred metres in altitude, the first steep pull eases towards the second alp, which is reached in another half an hour. The way between these alps grows more narrow, whilst above Zeznina Dadaint the path is in the open, above the treeline and picking a route first near the stream, then climbing in numerous tight zig-zags to the south. The cirque broadens; there are snow patches higher, and slopes of scree and rock.

After the zig-zags the way continues towards the head of the cirque. Off to the right is seen another hut, this one belonging to the military authorities. Soon after you come to the high mountain bowl with its cluster of tarns and tiny flowers and huge views out to the north, while blocking the basin to the south are the circling ridges of Piz Sursassa (2,968m), Spi da Laschadura (3,001m) and the long ridge that leads over several tops to Piz Macun (2,889m). Between Piz Sursassa and Spi di Laschadura the ridge dips to the pass of Fuorcletta Pitschna (2,839m) beyond which there is a steep descent possible to Zernez.

Route 90: Lavin (1,412m) - Guarda (1,653m) - Ardez (1,464m) - Ftan (1,633m) - Scuol (1,244m)

Grade:	1		
Distance:	17 kilometres		
Height gain:	241 metres	Height loss:	409 metres
Time:	4½-5 hours		

This is a truly delightful walk, the Lower Engadine equivalent of the *Sentiero panoramico* (Route 10) of the Val Bregaglia, and the *Via Engiadina* of the Upper Engadine (Route 40). Throughout the walk there are magnificent views down-valley and across to the mountains walling the southern side. There are flower meadows to wander through, and the classic villages of Guarda and Ardez to delay in, studying the fabulous old houses and their decorated walls, the cobbled squares, the narrow alleyways with views teasing at the far end of every one. Towards Ftan the castle of Tarasp can be seen perched on its cone of rock down in the valley, and as you start to descend towards Scuol, so it grows in stature, looking so picturesque with the shapely mountains of the Pisoc group forming a backcloth. The path is always easy, graded at a gentle angle for most of the way, and never flagging in interest. A highly recommended outing for all who enjoy tranquil mountain scenery.

For those who might consider the distance a little more than they'd choose for a single day's walk, Ardez comes practically halfway along the route, thereby giving the opportunity to break the walk into two separate day stages.

From Lavin station go beneath the roadway and onto the green hillside, taking the right fork of two tracks, curving round the slope to cross the lower reaches of Val Tuoi coming from the left. Cross the stream over a bridge to its left bank and follow round to join the main approach road to Guarda. This is reached in a little under one and a half hours from Lavin. (Allow yourself plenty of time to explore this classic village, although it really demands your full concentration, and half a day should be set aside specifically for this purpose.)

Ardez from the path to Ftan

There are two routes out of Guarda to choose from. One follows the unmade road leading from the upper end of Guarda's main street, and winds along the hillside to pass through the tiny hamlet of Bos-cha (1,664m) before reaching Ardez. The other takes a higher route and climbs uphill (on the Val Tuoi approach track) from the upper end of Guarda, then branches off to the right to work along the steep slopes, through forest then out again on an interesting tour of little alp clusters like Teas and Chöglias, before dropping down on the trail to Ardez.

Ardez also deserves a close study. Make a point of looking at the artistry of the Adam and Eve house in its main street; a unique feature dating from the 17th century.

Again, there are alternative ways to reach Ftan from Ardez; either of which will be found quite acceptable. The easier of the two follows the unmade hillside road from the eastern end of Ardez (traffic will only be met rarely along this road) and is a delightful belvedere with magnificent views along the valley stretching out below. It winds round the slopes, sometimes through forest, often through meadows

158

of flowers on a delightful course, until at last it leads directly into Ftan-Grond. The other route climbs higher above Ardez - the path begins near the church - and forks right to reach the ruins of Chanoua before curving left (northwards) in the mouth of Val Tasna a little above the unmade road. Various alternatives become available here. You could join the unmade road route, or climb by a track through the trees to gain the upper buildings of Ftan-Grond, or for the extra-energetic, divert a short way into Val Tasna, climb to Alp Laret high on its eastern wall, then slant over the spur of mountain to drop into Ftan. Consult the 1:50,000 scale map if the latter diversion is contem-plated.

Walk through Ftan-Grond (the western section of the village) and ignore the road heading off to the right, signposted Scuol, and instead, continue ahead into Ftan-Pitschen. From here a trail leads on a descending traverse of the steep hillside steadily down to Scuol in the valley, enjoying lovely views all the way.

Route 91:   Guarda (1,653m) - Tuoi Hut (2,250m)

Grade: 2
Distance: 7 kilometres
Height gain: 597 metres
Time: 2½ hours

Val Tuoi is one of my favourite Lower Engadine valleys, for so many reasons. Firstly, I suppose, for its surprise views, for Guarda gives no hint of the delights to be found in the valley whose entrance is so distorted by the steepness of the pastures rising immediately behind the village. Once in it, however, Piz Buin's great cone leans over the upper reaches with great character. Then there are the streams, ever-bubbling, chattering, racing through the meadows, swirling among the rocks and boulders. There are the larches that make a show of forest in the lower portion of the valley, but then there are the flowers in the meadows, on the rocks, beside the streams. Everywhere, colour, fragrance, soft tranquil vistas.

Snow lies deep at the head of the valley until July. Until then the hut is likely to be unattainable, but if you should be spending a holiday in the Engadine say, in June, I would urge you at least to wander as far as possible into Val Tuoi before you come to snow. June will display a glorious mass of flowers here, and a gentle amble among them will compensate for a reduced walk. And when you return down-valley towards Guarda, there will be more freshly laundered views to enthuse over as you look across the Engadine's deep trench to the southern wall of mountains.

The Tuoi hut belongs to the SAC's *Secziun Engiadina Bassa*, and is ideally situated for ascents of several neighbouring peaks, many of which rise beyond the Swiss-Austrian border which runs along the ridge heading the valley. There are several high glacier passes in that ridge, too, whose crossing would make an adventurous outing or two for the experienced and well-equipped party. The hut can sleep 66 people. Meals and drinks are available when the guardian is in occupation, which is from mid-July until the middle of October. It is also open for ski ascents for about six weeks from the middle of March each year.

Towards the upper end of Guarda's lovely village street a signpost directs the start of the walk up through meadows on a climbing path that is joined by a broader trail where the signpost reads: Alp Suot and Chamanna Tuoi. The track climbs on, but less steeply now, and leads into the mouth of Val Tuoi. As you swing into this, go up onto the grassy ridge above the track and enjoy the views back into the Engadine.

Follow the track through Val Tuoi, keeping above the eastern bank of the stream. There are patchy larch woods at first, then pastures, and at last a rougher terrain of boulders, rocks, and slopes of poor grass. After Alp Suot (2,018m) trade the broad track for a more narrow path forging straight ahead (there are alternative paths climbing up to the right, but these should be ignored). The path leads directly to Chamanna Tuoi, the SAC's hut, with Piz Buin looming overhead.

**Route 92: Guarda (1,653m) - Tuoi Hut (2,250m) -
               Furcletta (2,735m) - Val Tasna - Ardez (1,464m)**

Grade: 3
Distance: 20 kilometres
Height gain: 1,082 metres   Height loss: 1,271 metres
Time: 7-7½ hours

A long and demanding excursion, this could be broken by spending a night at the Tuoi hut, thereby making a two-day outing and gaining the additional pleasure of a night in remote surroundings. Both Val Tuoi and Val Tasna are delightful in themselves, and by the crossing of the Furcletta (in about 1½ hours from the hut) they can be effectively linked into this single trek. Immediately beyond the pass (made

The Adam and Eve House in Ardez, Lower Engadine

among screes and snow patches) the way descends into the feeder valley of Val d'Urezzas which leads into Val Tasna. It's a *Bergweg*, marked with red and white paint flashes where the path grows indistinct.

Take Route 91 from Guarda to the Tuoi hut. Furcletta lies a little north of east of the hut, between Piz da la Clavigliadas (2,983m) that sends out a projection from the ridge, and Piz Furcletta (2,894m). The route heads up pastureland north-eastwards following a stream that comes from a tiny pool. After about a quarter of an hour bear more to the right to go eastwards, climbing now towards, and over, scree and snow slopes, so to gain the pass. A magnificent view to Piz Buin is enlivened in the west by glaciers, snow and rock that together form the headwall of Val Tuoi. On the other side of the pass, the panorama includes more glacier, more snow, rock and deep-cut valley. To the left rise the big Silvretta peaks. Off towards the right all the land falls away to the Lower Engadine.

The descent from Furcletta into Val d'Urezzas is often over snow slopes in its upper reaches. Then down to find a path that follows the left bank of the main valley stream from the alp of Marangun d'Urezzas (2,273m) to its lower counterpart, Alp Urezzas (2,111m) in the mouth of the valley. Here the path is joined by another. Cross the stream and follow the right bank of the Tasna stream all the way down through the lovely green valley. It's a fine valley of woods and pastures, with alps on the hillsides and views ahead as you draw nearer the Engadine. As you leave Val Tasna, either drop onto the unmade road, or take the trail leading from it a little higher, going to the right. Both lead round to Ardez.

Other Routes from Val Tuoi:

Experienced, well-equipped mountain trekkers may well be tempted by prospects of breaching the international frontiers at the head of Val Tuoi. The following routes are almost climbers' ways, but given the necessary expertise to tackle glacier work, these suggestions are offered for adventurous days out in the mountains.

From the Tuoi hut westwards climb into the glacial corrie between Piz Buin and Piz Fliana, there to gain the Cudera Glacier and the *Silvretta Pass* (3,003m), then down the Silvretta Glacier to the SAC's *Silvretta Hut* (about 6 hours), and beyond to reach Klosters.

In Austria, the *Wiesbadner Hut* may be reached from Val Tuoi by climbing over *Fuorcla Vermunt* (2,798m) in the shadow of Piz Buin, then descending the broken Vermuntgletscher. Or over the high *Jamjoch* (3,078m) for a glacier descent to the *Jamtal Hut*, with prospects of making a circular tour by returning to Switzerland over *Pass Futschöl* (2,768m), dropping into Val Urschai, climbing through Val d'Urezzas and over *Furcletta* back to the Tuoi hut. This would make a superb two day circuit. Demanding, but rewarding. There's also *Fuorcla d'Anschatscha* linking the valleys of Tuoi and Lavinuoz to the west; not a glacier pass, but a somewhat difficult one that would give a long day's tour, Guarda to Lavin.

All in all, Val Tuoi is ideally positioned for a number of routes of varying degrees of commitment; from leisurely rambles among the flower meadows, to demanding climbs over crevassed glaciers and rock-guarded passes.

Route 93: Ardez (1,464m) - Val Sampuoir - Fuorcla Pedrus (2,814m) - Val Plavna - Fontana (1,402m)

Grade: 3
Distance: 22 kilometres
Height gain: 1,350 metres   Height loss: 1,412 metres
Time: 8½ hours

A long, strenuous yet scenic day's walking, this route links two fine valleys that run south of the Lower Engadine towards the National Park. In the high country at the head of both valleys there are prospects of sighting chamois and marmots.

From Ardez station take the road leading down to the river, cross over and follow a track leading into Val Sampuoir beyond. It leads through forest on the the left bank (west bank) of the stream, gaining height along the steep slopes. As the forest thins out, so you come to Alp Sampuoir, about two and a half hours from Ardez. Continue up-valley beside the stream, keeping with it when an alternative path leads up to the right towards a higher alp. Red and white paint flashes give assurance of the route. Cross the stream to bear slightly left where the valley's head is seen to be blocked by a tight cirque of mountains. In the centre of the cirque, the ridge makes a sharp right-angle at Piz Sampuoir. The pass, Fuorcla Pedrus, lies below this peak to the left, and is reached after about five hours of walking.

To the north of the pass the ridge rises in battlements of spires to Piz Plavna Dadaint, one of the most dramatic of peaks hereabouts, but seen to better advantage from points farther to the east. The route descends now quite steeply into the bowl of Pischa Dadaint, passing carefully round the cliffs that obstruct the central part of the corrie.

On reaching the foot of the slope, cross to the eastern side of the stream and find a path leading down to Alp Plavna (1½ hours from the pass). This path becomes more easily defined as it works its way down-valley, keeping company with the stream until after some time it leaves the bed of the valley and heads through forest on the right-hand side, becoming a track that leads into the sunny pastures of Fontana, with the castle of Tarasp seen rising ahead.

Take the Postbus from Fontana to Scuol or Ardez.

Route 94:. Ftan (1,633m) - Alp Valmala (1,979m)

Grade: 1-2
Distance: 7.5 kilometres
Height gain: 346 metres
Time: 2 hours

This walk serves as an introduction to the gentle greenery of Val Tasna, the glen that runs northward midway between Ardez and Ftan. In fact this walk can as easily be taken from either village. There is little difference in time or distance.

Take the unmade road that leads between Ftan and Ardez. It cuts back into the mouth of Val Tasna in order to cross the stream issuing from the valley. The footpath begins at this bridge and leads through forest with the stream running down on the left through its tight bed. From the start there is a hint of good things to come, and as you head deeper into the valley, so the promise is fulfilled. The track continues to follow the eastern bank of the stream all the way, with views up-valley towards the Augstenberg, across whose ridges runs the Austrian border. Alp Valmala is reached in something like an hour and a half from the valley's entrance. The valley tightens beyond it, then opens to the junction of Val d'Urezzas on the left, and Val Urschai forking right ahead.

Route 95:   Ftan (1,633m) - Pass Futschöl (2,768m) -
Jamtal Hut (2,165m)

Grade: 3
Distance: 18 kilometres
Height gain: 1,135 metres   Height loss: 603 metres
Time: 7 hours

The crossing of Pass Futschöl makes a convenient passage between
164

the Lower Engadine and the Austrian Tyrol, and enables a south-north traverse to be made of the Silvretta mountains without undue difficulty. The Jamtal Hut lies in a basin near the head of the Jamtal, and a further hour's walking down-valley would bring you to the village of Galtür, about 40 kilometres west of Landeck, in the Paznauntal.

Take Route 94 as far as Alp Valmala, then continue up-valley, still beside the stream, past the alp of Urschai which is found just beyond the junction with Val d'Urezzas on the left, so to reach the remote buildings of Marangun d'Urschai (2,210m) a little over three hours' walking time from Ftan. Here, cross the stream and climb steeply round the spur of Piz Futschöl, then bear left (north) over moraine and scree in a sharp pull up to the pass. (Reached in about 5½ hours from Ftan.) The peak of Augstenberg (3,230m) rises above your left shoulder, wearing little glacial shawls. Ahead stands the Fluchthorn across a cirque of glacier, snowfield and scree.

The continued marked trail takes you down to the centre of the little amphitheatre to find the main stream. Follow this on its right bank. It curves leftward and drops directly to the hut, which is found over-looking the long trench of the Jamtal.

Route 96: Ftan (1,633m) - Ardez (1,464m)

Grade:	1
Distance:	4 kilometres
Height loss:	169 metres
Time:	1¼ hours

An easy stroll, ideal for families with young children, this follows the unmade road that runs along the hillside some way above the valley. It is a quiet track with very little traffic; well worth strolling along, for the lovely views and the marvellous flower meadows it goes through. Now and then there are parallel footpaths through the meadows or woods, so enabling the road to be deserted for a while.

Ftan is divided into Grond and Pitschen. The road up from Scuol goes directly to Ftan-Grond, which is the larger, western part of the village. Follow the road leading through it, keeping the church on your right, and head south-westwards away from the village. The road goes up to a meadowland shelf, the track bordered by a wooden fence, but shortly after leaving the village, a footpath branches away left and skirts round to rejoin the road later. Early in the summer the meadows here are a mass of colour and fragrance. Alpine pastures at their very best.

As the track continues, so views open along the valley, but then it curves round to the right to cross the entrance to Val Tasna, and views are restricted by the spruce trees that border the road, but also by the projection of mountainside beyond. However, having crossed the stream pouring from Val Tasna, the track bears left and works its way round the hillside (here another footpath branches away to the right, also leading to Ardez, but by a higher route; equally worth taking) and once more the views become extensive. Both the track and the footpath lead directly to Ardez.

**Route 97: Scuol (1,244m) - Val Sinestra - Vna (1,602m) -
Tschlin (1,533m) - Vinadi (1,086m)**

Grade: 2
Distance: 28 kilometres
Height gain: 358 metres   Height loss: 516 metres
Time: 7½-8 hours

The *Panoramaweg Unterengadin* is another of those delightful hillside traverses so typical of this corner of Switzerland. Along the way there are several interesting and remote villages to wander through. There are meadows and forests, diversions made into side valleys, and always fine views to enjoy. Wandering as it does along the northern side of the valley, this route is almost constantly in the sun, so choose your day well, and take protective measures if you are susceptible to sunburn.

The walk begins on the edge of Scuol where the main Engadine road has a branch forking left for Sent. Near this road junction a footpath slants up the hillside to run parallel with, and a little uphill of, the road. It takes you directly to Sent village, a sunny spot with lovely views to the Engadine Dolomites opposite. Leaving Sent, the path again runs parallel with, and a little uphill of, the road (now unmade) which cuts along the hillside heading north-eastwards and curving round to enter Val Sinestra in forest shade. Both path and road travel some distance into this narrow shaft of a valley, and join again at a large Victorian spa hotel, the Kurhaus Val Sinestra. The road stops here. Cross the bridge over the river below the Kurhaus, and take the narrow path right, going through the forest, climbing steadily up the steep hillside, branching left where the path forks, so to cross through sloping pastures on the way to Vna, eventually reaching the tiny village perched high on the hillside with forest above and trees below,

166

and the Lower Engadine shafting away in the south.

Take the lower of two paths cutting away from the village street heading eastwards through more meadows. For some distance it traverses the hillsides far above the Engadine, past isolated barns and other farm buildings; cuts back to cross the Ruinains gorge at its most convenient point, then steadily loses height on the traverse approach to Tschlin, reached through pastures rich in alpine flowers.

From Tschlin to Vinadi the *Panoramaweg* at first loses a little height, then climbs to Pra Ground, from which point it maintains its height for a while, passing way above Martina through forest, and continuing through more forest above the gorge that squeezes the Inn's departure from Switzerland. The path then drops down into the gorge at Vinadi. From here a narrow road leads off to the duty-free haven of Samnaun. Postbuses serve this last remote corner.

Route 98:   Scuol (Motta Naluns (2,146m) - Prui (2,058m) - Ftan Pitschen (1,644m) - Scuol (1,244m)

Grade: 1-2
Distance: 9.5 kilometres
Height loss: 902 metres
Time: 2½ hours

By use of the gondola lift from Scuol to Motta Naluns an easy high-level walk and descent can be achieved, thereby giving the opportunity for the less-committed of mountain walkers to enjoy countryside that might otherwise remain out of bounds. On this walk there are numerous wild flower varieties to be seen, including a number of interesting alpine species on the upper hillsides.

The Motta Naluns cableway begins near Scuol railway station where there is adequate car parking space available. Take the lift to Motta Naluns; a ride of less than fifteen minutes. Take the footpath heading left on leaving the gondola upper station. The path wanders along the hillside terrace in a westerly direction with lovely views across the valley. But there are flowers at your feet that also deserve attention.

On reaching Prui (or Natéus, as it is sometimes known) there is a chair-lift coming up from Ftan. Go beyond this on a continuing path which leads towards Alp Laret, but shortly after Prui bear left and drop down in loops to cut through the forest trees on the descent to Ftan. From the village take the path signposted to Scuol which leads down through flower-splashed meadows, and with those delightful views overlooking the castle of Tarasp in the valley below. So to reach

167

Scuol once more.

Other Routes from Scuol:
Scuol is well-situated for a number of very fine walking tours, but some of these may best be taken from outlying villages or valleys first reached by either Postbus or car. However, there are short and easy rambles to be had in the surrounding meadows that grant magnificent low-valley views. Try, for example, crossing the Inn to its southern side and wandering up to *Bain Jonnair* (1,423m) in the ever-fragrant forests, then head along westwards to *San Jon* and on the S-charl road towards the *Clemgia Gorge*, which can then be crossed by a footpath leading round to Fontana.

Fontana's undulating pastures have good paths leading through them, too, with *Lej da Tarasp* and *Lej Nair* making focal points for picnics and photographs. Wander among the meadows and woods here with photogenic views of Tarasp Castle.

Or above Scuol on the northern side of the valley. From the Motta Naluns gondola cableway there are other walks available, beside that already suggested via Prui to Ftan. There are high routes to *Piz Champatsch* (2,919m); to *Alp Laret*, or eastwards to *Sent*. And variations on a theme. Study the local map and numerous ideas will form in your mind; or visit Scuol Information Office and enquire about organised guided walks which are arranged during the summer and are free of charge for those staying in the town.

Route 99: S-charl (1,810m) - Alp Astras (2,135m)

Grade: 1
Distance: 7 kilometres
Height gain: 325 metres
Time: 2 hours

The long S-charl valley leads to a hidden region of soft pastures, lush inner glens with tumbling streams and forests and remote alps. The National Park's north-eastern boundary runs along its lower reaches, and this gives the opportunity for those staying in S-charl village to explore a valley or two of the Park. But so varied are the immediate valleys radiating from the village, that a walking holiday based here would be worthwhile considering. There are hotels and *pensions* and *matratzenlager* accommodation available. On the other hand, S-charl is served by Postbus from Scuol, while a car approach through the valley will not add too much of a burden to the day's walking. Motorists should park their cars immediately before entering the village. There is an unsurfaced area set aside for this on the right-hand side of the road. (Incidentally, the valley is closed off by snow from the rest of the Engadine during winter, and even in June there are often large banks of snow towering on either side of the unmade road.)

For this route, wander through the village heading east on a broad track that has forest bordering it on the left, and a boulder-littered meadow on the right with the stream rushing through it. The track steadily gains height, sometimes above, and sometimes beside, the stream. It curves gently towards the south, then crosses the stream on a wooden bridge, with a more narrow path diverting away to the left. Cross this bridge on the continuing trail that has views across the valley to a decaying alp hut. The way presses on above the stream. Soon above the path will be seen a collection of alp buildings, reached by another path straying away from ours to the right. This is alp Praditschöl (2,131m); a fine example of Swiss alpine vernacular architecture, with dwelling house, cattle sheds and milking parlour set above a slope of rock and grass. The roofs are wooden shingled, the guttering also made of wood, and with lovely bow-topped windows in its side-roofs.

Continue up-valley to where the Val Tamangur (the upper reaches of the Val S-charl) widens and has a moorland quality about it. At a junction of paths sits Alp Astras, enjoying pleasant views up and down the valley, with busy streams around. This alp has another collection of well-designed buildings in an enchanting setting. Look out for marmots here.

Marmot

**Route 100: S-charl (1,810m) - Alp Astras (2,135m) -
Fuorcla Funtana da S-charl (2,393m) -
Ofen Pass (2,149m)**

Grade: 2
Distance: 13 kilometres
Height gain: 583 metres   Height loss: 244 metres
Time: 3½ hours

An extension of Route 99, this walk makes it possible to link the
S-charl valley with either Val Müstair, falling east from the Ofen Pass,
or the Engadine via Zernez. There is a Postbus service to both valleys
from the summit of the pass (Süsom Givè), and accommodation to be
had at Il Fuorn a little below the pass towards Zernez.

Follow Route 99 to Alp Astras. Here a signpost marks the beginning
of a path which forks away to the right, climbing up the rough hillside. It is a clear path, easy and well-defined, and it brings you to the
pass of Fuorcla Funtana da S-charl about two and a half hours after
leaving S-charl village. The path divides a little way beyond the actual
pass; the left-hand trail going to Alp da Munt and Tschierv; the right-
hand fork being the route to the Ofen Pass. Both are clear and offer no
difficulty.

**Route 101: S-charl (1,810m) - Alp Astras (2,135m) -
Pass da Costainas (2,251m) - Lü (1,920m) -
Santa Maria (1,375m)**

Grade: 2
Distance: 20 kilometres
Height gain: 441 metres   Height loss: 876 metres
Time: 5 hours

This is a variation of Route 100; another way of linking Val S-charl
with Val Müstair, that delightful, soft, velvety warm Italianate valley
with the international (Swiss-Italian) frontier just beyond Santa
Maria. Santa Maria itself has a fabulous old church well worth
visiting. Postbuses return from here to the Engadine over the Ofen
Pass.

Wander as far as Alp Astras (Route 99), but instead of bearing right
here, as for Route 100, continue along the valley spreading before you,
keeping with the bed of the glen as it swings to the right, then climb to
the narrow dip of a pass in about forty minutes from Alp Astras.
Through Pass da Costainas the way divides. The right-hand alter-

native heads down to Tschierv, the left-hand fork (our route) drops down to Alp Champatsch (2,136m). From here the way slopes off among trees to reach the little hamlet of Lü. A narrow road heads down into Val Müstair, but a hillside path slants away among forest shade to the left and eventually comes to Santa Maria.

Route 102: S-charl (1,810m) - Fuorcla Funtana da S-charl (2,393m) - Tschierv (1,660m) - Pass da Costainas (2,251m) - S-charl

Grade.	2
Distance:	26 kilometres
Height gain:	1,174 metres Height loss: 1,174 metres
Time:	7 hours

By combining the two previous routes a long circuit can be achieved, thereby giving a very full day's exercise, and in so doing gaining a wide variety of experiences and mountain perspectives.

Follow Route 100 as far as the pass of Fuorcla Funtana da S-charl, and where the path forks just to the south of it, take the left-hand route via Alp da Munt (2,213m) to the hamlet of Tschierv above the Ofen Pass-Val Müstair road. Now bear left to enter the knuckle valley cutting back a little from the main valley, to rise steadily through forest on the climb to gain Pass da Costainas. Once through this pass follow the trail down-valley to reach Alp Astras (in effect reversing Route 101), and continue along the path leading back to S-charl.

Route 103: S-charl (1,810m) - Alp Sesvenna (2,098m)

Grade:	1
Distance:	2.5 kilometres
Height gain:	288 metres
Time:	1 hour

Running to the north-east of S-charl village is a lovely glen; the Val Sesvenna. It's a green and pleasant vale blocked by attractive mountains. There are forests at its entrance and meadows within. There's a fine river flowing through it, dancing and flashing in globules of spray across its stony bed, and in the early summer particularly, it makes a great place for a picnic. It is the unannounced splendour of glens such as this that makes a visit to the Alps so pleasurable, for to discover quiet back-country valleys is as satisfying as meeting for the first time one of the much-publicised big-mountain viewpoints. To the lover of

Val Sesvenna, near S-charl

mountain scenery, Val Sesvenna will be hailed as a minor masterpiece.

From the village square in S-charl take the lane heading left, past a fountain gushing into a trough, and follow the track beyond a few neat houses along the true left bank of the river (eastern side). After a short distance, cross over by way of a wooden bridge and bear right to wander among flowers and trees and shrubs, as far as the little Alp Sesvenna, with its hut nestling here beneath the ridge running from Piz Madlain to Piz d'Immez. There is another alp, higher in the valley to the east and linked by a continuing path in about forty minutes; but it is no more attractive in its setting than this first one, where in early

Ibex

morning and evening it is possible to see ibex grazing.

Route 104: S-charl (1,810m) - Alp Tavrü (2,121m)

Grade: 1-2
Distance: 4.5 kilometres
Height gain: 311 metres
Time: 1½ hours

This short and easy walk leads into Val Tavrü whose entrance lies a little way down-valley from the village. Although heavily forested at its entrance a good path leads through and up to this alp, where there is a large colony of marmots.

Walk down-valley from S-charl on the unmade road heading north-west, and then cross the river by way of a small bridge seen just before the Tavrü stream joins the main Clemgia river. Follow the path beyond as it leads clearly through the forest and into Val Tavrü. On emerging from the forest it makes a sharp turn to the right and climbs up to Alp Tavrü.

Other Routes from S-charl:

For a fine walk in the *Val Mingèr* to Il Foss, see Route 83 under the National Park section. This is a three-hour walk.

A 5-6 hour outing could be adopted by taking the path just up-valley from the village, across the Clemgia stream by way of a bridge, then up to *Mot Mezdi* through the Jürada Forest. From Mot Mezdi across meadows forming an easy ridge, and then along to the summit of *Piz dal Geier* with its far vistas of the Ortler group of mountains.

In the Val Sesvenna one could make a long day's journey over *Fuorcla Sesvenna* (2,819m) to the head of the Italian Valle Slingia. From there a choice of routes gives the opportunity to either descend south into the Adige, or to climb north-westwards through *Alpe di Slingia* and over the pass above it back into Switzerland, there to descend through *Val d'Uina* to regain the Lower Engadine at Sur En.

Still wandering through a portion of Val Sesvenna, another high crossing could be made of the pass in the ridge running between Piz Madlain and Piz d'Immez. This leads onto a glacier, which in turn allows access to the *Lischana Hut* to the north of Piz San Jon.

One more route linking the S-charl valley with the lower Val Müstair, in this instance just across the Italian border, goes up-valley from S-charl, then branches away from the main trail to pass through Alp Plazer, then over the saddle of *Cruschetta* on a clear path, to descend into Val d'Avigna.

Route 105: Sent (1,430m) - Kurhaus Val Sinestra (1,521m) -
Griosch (1,817m) - Vna (1,602m) - Ramosch (1,231m)

Grade: 2
Distance: 17 kilometres
Height gain: 387 metres   Height loss: 586 metres
Time: 4-4½ hours

The Val Sinestra is a major valley feeding into the lower reaches of the Engadine between the hillside villages of Sent and Ramosch. It is so deep at its entrance that no crossing is possible in its first four kilometres, save for a bridge that takes the Engadine highway over the river just below Ramosch. However, up-valley the mountain walls constrict into a dark gorge where the Kurhaus stands overlooking the river. Here a foot crossing can be made, overshadowed by tall and elegant forest trees. Beyond the gorge the valley begins to spread itself, thus allowing space for a few pastures and remote summer hamlets. This walk explores part of the Val Sinestra, visits some of the little hamlets, and returns to the Lower Engadine by way of Vna and Ramosch.

If you have motor transport, it would be possible to drive as far as the Kurhaus (limited parking space) and save about 1½ hours of walking. But in this case it will be necessary to cut back from Vna to retrieve the car, thus abandoning the final section of the walk to

Ramosch. If, however, the complete walk is planned, catch a Postbus back to Scuol or Sent from Ramosch.

Take the narrow lane leading from Sent along the hillside and into forest where the Val Sinestra begins. Along the first part of this lane there are wonderful views along and across the Engadine; a superb belvedere. At the Kurhaus in Val Sinestra go down to the river and cross over by way of a bridge to the eastern side. Follow the path left as it scrambles alongside the river with the dense forest crowding on both sides of the valley. Several times the narrow path crosses and recrosses the river before coming onto a drivable track about forty minutes from the Kurhaus. The track comes to a desolate region of scree and ancient moraines where you will see a collection of curious formations of rock towers with larger stones balanced on top. These are formed by weathering of the soft 'tower' rock, while the harder 'table' blocks have resisted a similar degree of erosion.

Shortly after passing these you come to the tiny collection of farm buildings known as Zuort. Refreshments are available here. From this point the valley becomes more open and quite lovely with alp huts higher amid lush pastures. The path continues up-valley, crosses the stream again and slants up to reach the hamlet of Griosch, with its fine valley views. Now return along the high track that traverses the hillside going south towards the Engadine. You pass through Pra San Peder; a single file of old alp buildings gazing across the valley. The belvedere track is always interesting with its distant views, and takes about 1¼ hours to reach Vna. A superb setting for a little village. From here a narrow road leads down from Vna in long hillside loops to Ramosch.

Route 106: Sent (1,430m) - Val Sinestra - Zuort (1,711m) - Alp Pra San Flurin (2,080m)

Grade: 2
Distance: 11 kilometres
Height gain: 650 metres
Time: 3½ hours

Halfway along Val Sinestra a glaciated side valley curves in from the west. This is Val Laver, in whose pastures are contained several alps. This walk explores the valley and visits these alps, the last of which is that of Pra San Flurin.

Take Route 105 as far as the farm buildings of Zuort. From this point a track swings in loops up the wooded hillside to the west (left) in order to gain entry to Val Laver. The track remains on the north side of the stream, skirts an open meadow, then branches into the valley to pass the first alp. Beyond this the path forks. The right-hand path slants up the hillside to the alp of Muranza (2,074m); straight ahead another path leads to Alp Era; while the left-hand trail drops down to the stream, crosses it, then heads west again also to reach Alp Era (2,045m). Take the left-hand option. Continuing along the southern side of the stream, the path soon reaches Alp Pra San Flurin by recrossing to the north bank.

At the head of the valley Fuorcla Champatsch (2,730m) crosses the ridge between Piz Nair and Piz Champatsch, and has a route that drops steeply down on the far side to Scuol. (About 8½ hours from Sent.)

As an alternative return to Sent, rather than retrace the complete uphill route, follow the downhill path from Pra San Flurin, but where it branches off to cross the stream to the north bank, continue ahead on a trail that leads into forest soon after. (Another path branches right and goes up to yet another alp, Alp Patschai.) Keep with the forest path as it curves into Val Sinestra. It will take you back to the Kurhaus Val Sinestra, or without dropping to the road here, go straight on along the hillside until it meets again with the road at Chavriz Grond.

Route 107: Sent (1,430m) - Val Sinestra -
Cuolmen d'Fenga (2,608m) - Heidelberger Hut (2,264m)

Grade: 3
Distance: 18 kilometres
Height gain: 1,178 metres   Height loss: 344 metres
Time: 5½-6 hours

A long day's outing, this walk is interesting from several angles. It is, of course, extremely varied in its scenery. There are a number of little alps to pass through; the saddle of Cuolmen d'Fenga is botanically very rich, and the descent to the Heidelberger Hut, whilst still in Switzerland, is nonetheless geographically Austrian. (Even the hut does not belong to the SAC, but to the DAV (Deutscher Alpenverein), despite its being in Swiss territory.) The Val Fenga becomes the Austrian Fimbertal little more than two kilometres from the hut, and this in turn flows into the Paznauntal at Ischgl.

Follow directions as for Route 105 as far as the little alp hamlet of Griosch (1,817m - about 2½ hours from Sent). The valley stretches ahead with an obvious trail running along the eastern side of the stream. Continue along this, crossing and recrossing the stream where necessary for some three kilometres beyond Griosch to where the valley divides. Head left here, following the stream on its south bank on a marked path leading to Alp Chöglias. The path climbs on to reach the saddle of Cuolmen d'Fenga which marks the watershed. Through the pass the route shortly swings right to descend the slopes directly to the hut, which is to be found on the far side of the stream.

Other Routes in Val Sinestra:
Beginning at Ramosch a long day's hike goes to Samnaun; almost due north of Ramosch, but blocked by a contortion of ridges. The route leads first up to Vna, then along the hillside terrace path towards Griosch before branching away to the right to enter Val Tiatscha via Alp Pradgiant. At the head of this valley, *Fuorcla Maisas* (2,848m) breaches the ridge and gives access to the Maisas valley down which the path runs to *Samnaun* village. (Allow 7-7½ hours for this. Samnaun has plenty of hotels and *pensions,* and Postbus service back into the Engadine.)

Another demanding day's exercise can be had on a circuit of *Piz Arina* above Vna. This sentry peak stands guard at the entrance to Val Sinestra, and its summit captures spectacular panoramas. A circuitous path leads round it on green hillsides and over the pass of *Fuorcla Pradatsch.* A diversion can be made up to the summit at 2,828 metres; for the full circuit allow 8½ hours, Ramosch to Ramosch.

Appendix A: Useful Addresses

Swiss National Park Information
   Office
National Parkhaus
7530 Zernez
Switzerland

Information Offices:

Swiss National Tourist Office
Swiss Centre
1 New Coventry Street
London W1V 8EE

P.O. Box 215
Commerce Court
Toronto
Ontario
M5L 1E8
Canada

104 South Michigan Avenue
Chicago
Il 60603
USA

608 Fifth Avenue
New York
NY 10020
USA

250 Stockton Street
San Francisco
CA 94108
USA

Map Suppliers:

McCarta Ltd
122 Kings Cross Road
London WC1X 9DS

Edward Stanford Ltd
12-14 Long Acre
London WC2

The Map Shop
15 High Street
Upton-upon Severn
Worcs. WR8 0HJ

Rand McNally Map Store
10 East 53rd Street
New York
USA

Pacific Travellers
529 State Street
Santa Barbara
CA 93101
USA

Maps are also available from the Swiss
National Tourist Office.

Appendix B: Bibliography

Climbing Guides:
West Col Productions (Goring, Reading, Berks RG8 9AA, England) have published three climbers' guides to mountain areas included within the region covered by this book. They are as follows:

1. *Bernina Alps* by Collomb and Talbot - for the main snow summits, but also including several lesser peaks outlying the Bernina massif.

2. *Bregaglia East* by Collomb - for the Forno, Albigna, Allievi and Disgrazia areas.

3. *Bregaglia West* by Collomb - covering the Scioras, Cengalo, Badile and Trubinasca groups.

Walking:
Very little has hitherto appeared in English covering the walking potential of the Engadine and neighbouring valleys, but the following book makes a splendid introduction to the Bernina and Bregaglia areas. Long out of print, it may be obtainable through local libraries.

4. *Walking in the Alps* by J.H.Walker (Oliver & Boyd 1951).

General:
Numerous books about the Alps in general, and Switzerland in particular, include sections on the Engadine. Perhaps the most interesting, from a true mountaineering point of view, is the autobiography of Christian Klucker, foremost guide of the valley who lived nearly all his life in Val Fex (he is buried in the churchyard there) and who did much pioneering work in the Bregaglia, as well as numerous ascents of a classic nature among the Bernina peaks from the 1870's until the 1920's. Again, this book is long out of print, but should be available on request from your local library.

5. *Adventures of an Alpine Guide* by Christian Klucker (John Murray 1932).

National Park:
The National Park Authority in Switzerland has published many books and pamphlets to promote the Park in all its many aspects. Little, however, appears in English. The following titles either have an English language edition, or are multi-lingual publications with a section of English text, and are recommended. It may be possible to obtain them through the Swiss National Tourist Office, or failing that, direct from the National Parkhaus in Zernez.

6. *Through the Swiss National Park* (A Scientific Guide) - this hardback editions deals with the geology, hydrology, flora and fauna etc. of the Park. It is illustrated and comes with a 1:50,000 scale map of the National Park.

7. *Short Guide to the Swiss National Park* - a slim illustrated guide, including brief descriptions of walks within the Park. It also has a map included.

8. *Parc Naziunal Svizzer - Nature Trail* - a multi-lingual guide to the Park's nature trail, illustrated with line drawings.

Alpine Flowers:

Numerous illustrated guides have appeared in recent years depicting the magnificent variety of wild flowers to be found in the Alps. Of the two books listed below, the first is a soft-covered pocket guide that will easily fit into the rucksack of any flower-loving enthusiast, while the second is a splendidly produced hardback that contains a section giving details of where to find certain plants within the Engadine region. I would also draw the reader's attention to the *Bulletins* of the Alpine Garden Society which often contain articles specifically relating to the wild flowers of various parts of the Alps.

9. *The Alpine Flowers of Britain and Europe* by C. Grey-Wilson (Collins 1979).

10. *Mountain Flower Holidays in Europe* by L. Bacon (Alpine Garden Society 1979).

Nigritella nigra

Appendix C: Glossary of German & Romansch Terms

The following glossary lists a few words likely to be found on maps, in village streets or in foreign-language tourist information leaflets. It is no substitute for a pocket dictionary, but will hopefully be of some use.

German	Romansch	English
Abhang	spuonda	slope
Alp	alp	high pasture
Alpenblume	flur alpina	alpine flower
Alpenverein		alpine club
Alphütte	chamanna d'alp	mountain hut
Auskunft		information
Aussicht	la vista	view
Bach	ova	stream
Bahnhof		railway station
Berg	muntagna	mountain
Bergführer		mountain guide
Berggasthaus		mountain inn or lodging
Bergpass	cuomen or fuorcla	pass
Bergschrund		crevasse between a glacier & rock wall
Bergsteiger		mountaineer
Bergwanderer		mountain walker
Bergweg		mountain path
Blatt		map sheet
Brücke	punt	bridge
Dorf	cumin	village
Drahtseilbahn		cable-car
Ebene	planüra	plain
Feldweg	via champestra, stradella or senda	meadowland path
Fels	crippel, spelm	rock wall or slope
Fussweg		footpath
Gasthaus or gasthof		inn or lodging house
Gaststube		common room
Gemse	chamuotsch	chamois
Gletscher	vadret	glacier
Gletscherspalte	sfessa da vadret	crevasse
Grat	crasta, fil or spi	ridge
Grüss Gott or Gruetzi	allegra	greetings
Haltestelle		bus stop
Heilbad		spa, or hot springs

German	Romansch	English
Hirsch	tschierv	red deer
Horn	piz	horn, peak
Hügel	muot, muotta or collina	hill
Hütte	chamanna	mountain hut
Hüttenruhe		quiet time (in huts)
Jugendherberge		Youth Hostel
Kamm	craista	crest or ridge
Kapelle		chapel
Karte		map
Kirche		church
Klamm		gorge
Landschaft		landscape
Landstrasse	stradun	high road
Lawine	laviner	avalanche
Lebensmittel		grocery
Leicht		easy
Links		left
Matratzenlager		dormitory
Moräne		moraine
Murmeltier	muntanella	marmot
Nebenstrasse		second-class road or side street
Nord		north
Ost		east
Pass	fuorcla	pass
Pfad	senda	path
Quelle	funtana	spring
Rechts		right
Reh	chavriöl	roe deer
Sattel	fuorcla	saddle
Schlafraum		bedroom
Schloss	chastè	castle
Schlucht	chavorgia	gorge
See	lej or lei	lake
Strasse	via	road or street
Stunde		hour
Sud		south
Tal	vallada or val	valley
Tobel	vallun	wooded gorge
Touristenlager		tourist accommodation
Unfall		accident
Unterkunft		accommodation

German	Romansch	English
German	*Romansch*	*English*
Verkehrsverien		tourist office
Wald		forest
Wanderweg		footpath
Wasser	aua	water
Weide	pas-chura or pascul	pasture
West		west
Wildbach		torrent
Zeltplatz		campsite
Zimmer		room
- frei		vacancies

Chamois

CICERONE PRESS GUIDE BOOKS
TO WALKS AND CLIMBS IN EUROPE

FRANCE
- THE TOUR OF MONT BLANC — *Andrew Harper*
- TOUR OF THE OISANS — *Andrew Harper*
- WALKING THE FRENCH ALPS: GR5 — *Martin Collins*
- THE CORSICAN HIGH LEVEL ROUTE: GR20 — *Alan Castle*

FRANCE/SPAIN
- WALKS AND CLIMBS IN THE PYRENEES — *Kev Reynolds*

SWITZERLAND
- WALKS IN THE ENGADINE — *Kev Reynolds*

AUSTRIA/GERMANY
- MOUNTAIN WALKING IN AUSTRIA — *Cecil Davies*
- KING LUDWIG WAY — *Fleur and Colin Speakman*
- THE KALKALPEN TRAVERSE — *Alan Proctor*
- KLETTERSTEIG - Scrambles in the Northern Limestone Alps — *Paul Werner*

ITALY
- ALTA VIA - High Level Walks in the Dolomites — *Martin Collins*
- VIA FERRATA: Scrambles in the Dolomites — *Frass/Höffler/Werner*
- CLASSIC CLIMBS IN THE DOLOMITES — *Dinoia and Casari*
- ITALIAN ROCK: Selected climbs in Northern Italy — *Al Churcher*

GREECE
- MOUNTAINS OF GREECE: A Walkers' Guide — *Tim Salmon*

MALLORCA
- WALKING IN MALLORCA — *June Parker*

More titles are added to the list every year. If what you want is not listed, it may be in production.

Cicerone Press are specialist publishers of books for walkers, climbers and all lovers of the outdoors. The books listed above form part of those available:- walking and climbing in Britain, general books on topics such as weather and first aid, cartoon books etc. Send s.a.e. for current catalogue and price list to:

CICERONE PRESS, 2 Police Square, Milnthorpe, Cumbria, LA7 7PY

SWITZERLAND

BERN
o

ST. MORITZ
o

FLÜ

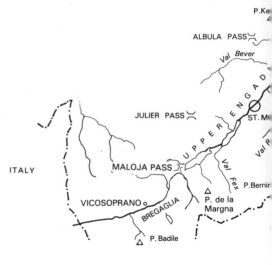

P.Ke

ALBULA PASS ⪥

Val *Bever*

U P P E R   E N G A D

JULIER PASS ⪥

ST. M(

Val R

ITALY

Val Fex

MALOJA PASS ⪤

P.Bernir

VICOSOPRANO o

BREGAGLIA

△ P. de la
Margna

△ P. Badile